A PRIMER TO ANTITRUST LAW AND REGULATORY POLICY

Kenneth M. Parzych

UNIVERSITY PRESS OF AMERICA

LANHAM • NEW YORK • LONDON

University Press of America,® Inc.

4720 Boston Way
Lanham, MD 20706

3 Henrietta Street
London WC2E 8LU England

Printed in the United States of America

British Cataloging in Publication Information Available

Library of Congress Cataloging in Publication Data

Parzych, Kenneth M., 1942-
A primer to antitrust law and regulatory policy.

Includes index.
1. Antitrust law—United States. I. Title.
KF1649.P37 1987 343.73'072 86-26754
347.30372
ISBN 0-8191-5785-6 (alk. paper)
ISBN 0-8191-5786-4 (pbk. : alk. paper)

All University Press of America books are produced on acid-free paper which exceeds the minimum standards set by the National Historical Publication and Records Commission.

To my wife, Mary,

And my children, Tim, Kevin, Dan, Patty,

And to my parents

OUTLINE

A PRIMER TO ANTITRUST LAW AND REGULATORY POLICY

Chapter One: INTRODUCTION AND ANALYSIS OF MARKET STRUCTURES

Chapter Two: ECONOMIC CONCENTRATION: ITS CAUSES AND EFFECTS

Chapter Three: THE ANTITRUST LAWS AND ENFORCEMENT

LISTING OF ILLUSTRATIONS AND TABLES

PREFACE

Our nation's antitrust initiative and regulatory policy has evolved to support and preserve the fundamental characteristics of the American capitalist economic system. While the free enterprise, market-oriented ideology characterizes the economic framework of many nations, it has assumed a very unique form within the United States. As a supportive response to the unique American capitalist experience, our nation's regulatory policy is equally different in many ways from the policy directives of other nations.

This book seeks to provide a basic and concise introduction to our nation's antitrust policy. In addition to examining the regulatory statutes and their various provisions, it introduces a limited review of judicial litigation to provide the reader with a perspective of the interpretation and jurisdictional application of the law.

I have purposefully sought to avoid having this work become encyclopedic. Rather, emphasis has been placed upon a selected number of judicial proceedings which provide a readable balance and re-inforce the legislative and judicial thrust of the law to the reader. A brief review of traditionally defined market structures is introduced, followed by an analysis of market concentration within the economy. The relationship between various types of barriers-to-entry and the structural characteristics of industry markets is examined.

In addition to a review of the antitrust laws and their judicial interpretation, there is an examination of additional statutes which have impeded and eroded the incidence of competition within various sectors of the economy.

There is a review of merger activity and an examination of the international jurisdiction of the nation's antitrust laws. Domestic firms engaged in international commerce and foreign companies that seek to penetrate the domestic market are subject to the regulatory restraints of the nations's regulatory policy.

While concise and brief, I would hope that the book provides a sufficiently detailed and meaningful understanding of our nation's antitrust policy. It is intended to be an informative reference for the business community and of substantative value for students matriculated in economics and business administration courses.

I am thankful to many individuals who have encouraged and challenged me during my years of academic preparation and professional affiliations in higher education. My colleagues at Eastern Connecticut State University have been very supportive and have been a source of continued encouragement.

Most importantly, it is the constant encouragement and loving support of my wife, Mary, and children, Tim, Kevin, Dan, and Patty, that have ensured the work's completion.

CHAPTER ONE

INTRODUCTION AND ANALYSIS OF MARKET STRUCTURE

Capitalism is a unique economic system that has adaptably survived and generally flourished for over two centuries. Most commonly identified with the Western World and notably the United States, it has been uniquely adapted to conform and compliment the different political and socio-economic conditions of many diverse nations.

Formalized in the writings of Adam Smith, the contemporary capitalist system traces its beginnings as a critical response to the early mercantilist doctrine. Mercantilism, as a distinct political and economic ideology, flourished throughout Europe for several centuries. It was characterized by a ruling monarch and very complete directive controls over all commercial and business activities.

It's ultimate objective and the measure of a nation's wealth was the increased stock of gold. Commonly referred to as Bullionism, it sought to ensure a continued favorable balance-of-trade from which its gold stock would grow, and assumedly, the nation's wealth. To further this objective, it colonized the "New World" from which inexpensive resources were extracted for domestic manufacture and exportation. Additionally, to maintain low production costs and competitive export prices, it maintained controls over the manufacturing process and domestic consumption among the native population. In sum, it contributed to the constant misery of the populace.

It was within this rigid ideological and institutional setting that the embryonic seeds of the market system evolved. In rejecting the mercantilist philosophy, early capitalism emphasized the increased production and exchange of goods and services as the barometer of a nation's wealth. Resources would be allocated into production, in anticipation of demand, and finished goods would be distributed into consumption on the basis of a market determined price. The concept of a functioning market mechanism, unrestrained by direct government intervention, was to be the distinguishing feature of early capitalism. Equally, the private ownership of resources, nature and man-made, to be used and managed for personal gain as a reward of risk-taking was assured to be a desirable and necessary incentive to ensure growth. Thus, the market system is notably motivated by the efforts of individuals to secure their personal economic gains from which the interests of the entire populace and the productive wealth of the nation will be ensured. Individuals will work productively to maximize their financial rewards from which they establish their material living standard, and businesses will equally seek to optimize their profit levels by providing a saleable product or service.

Unbounded faith was placed in the heralded benefits of a functioning market process as both an allocative and distributive mechanism. Assuming the existence of competition, the incidence of firm rivalry would seemingly ensure that resources would be allocated into the production process at efficient least cost and that finished products would be distributed into final consumption on a competitive, least price basis.

Within this ideal competitive market framework, it was assumed that government would not have to assume any significant interventionist role. Beyond the need to ensure the nation's defensive security, it was preferable for government to maintain a "laissez faire" approach and to minimize any form of controls or directives over economic activities and commercial transactions.

Modern capitalism has adaptably evolved and assumed distinct features which do not approximate this utopian historical market mode. Equally, the system has and continues to be haunted by the early criticisms levied against it. Most notably, the socialist criticism regarding the equitableness of its distributive process and the Marxian attack on it's inherent exploitive tendencies. Additionally, others have suggested that the system inevitably evolves into a structural situation that will contribute to its self destruction. Specifically, that this Darwinian principle applied to economics (The Fittest Survive) will contribute eventually to the elimination of meaningful competition and result in a structurally monopolized economy. While technological advance and innovations have historically contributed to the introduction of new products and thus the creation of new industries, it is the opinion of many observers that the classical preception of competition has withered to be replaced by a structurally monopolistic market environment. It is within this context that government assumed an increased and directive role in the regulation of business. Thus, the justified rationale to legislate antitrust laws and regulate business behavior is to approximate and preserve a competitive market environment.

CLASSICAL COMPETITIVE MODEL:

The classical definition of the pure competitive market structure forms the underlying foundation from which the functioning market mechanism operates under the Capitalist economic system. Commonly referred to as "atomistic" competition, it assumes the existence of a large number of relatively small-sized firms that are producing a similar and undifferentiated product. Since the products are standardized, consumers readily substitute their purchases of one product for others among the many producers. Because of this exceptionally high degree of product substitutability, the individual demand is very (perfectly) elastic in nature. This characteristic implies that consumers would readily and sensitively respond to any differences in prices among the firms. Thus, individual firms are unable to manage or effect their individual product price and sell their output at the determined price within the market. In sum, they are price-takers, at the mercy of the market, and are unable to individually manipulate supply or demand conditions.

Additionally, the competitive model is characterized by low or non-prohibitive barriers-to-entry which ensures that new firms are able to successfully enter the industry with relative ease. It is this condition that results in long-run adjustments within the market that contribute to productive least-cost efficiency and a least-cost determined price for the consumer.

Fig. 1.

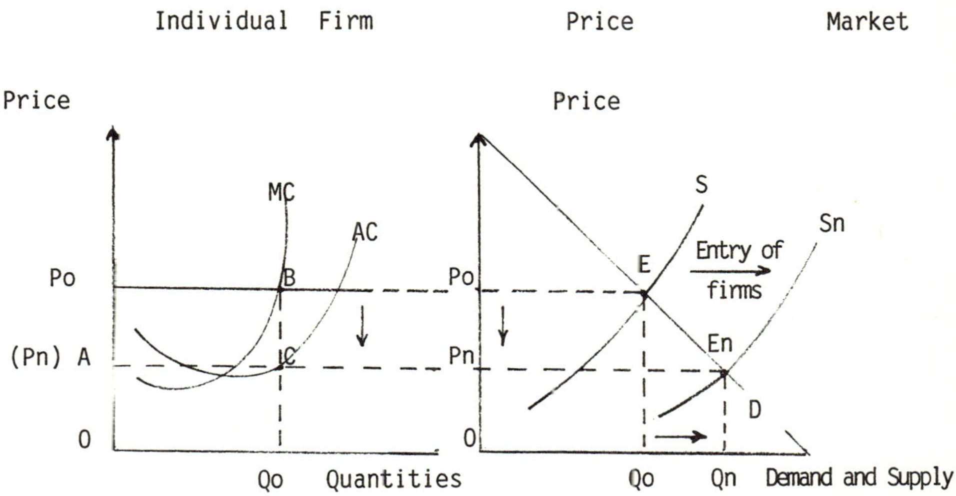

Fig. 1. depicts the initial market determined price of 0 Po. The individual firm sells its product at that price and maximizes profits (MC=MR) in producing and selling the quantity 0Qo.

In this illustration, the representative competitive firm is incurring an incremental economic profit of A-PO (the amount by which price exceeds average cost at a level of output 0Qo. Total economic profits approximate the area APoBC. (Unit Profit (APo) times quantity 0Qo).

This level of firm and total industry profitability will attract new enterprising firms to enter the market which will expand total market supply from S to Sn. The increase in supply will result in a new market equilibrium from E to En, and contribute to a lower determined market price from Po to Pn. This lower price, the new long-run adjusted price for the individual firm, now approximates MC and the minimum cost of producing the product. Under these conditions, the representative firm is now incurring a normal profit in which its total revenue covers its operational costs and additionally ensures a sufficient return above recordable expenses to reflect a reward for risk-taking and the incentive to sustain the production effort.

Note that this long-run competitive market adjustment is intended to ensure that the ultimate product price will be equated with minimum average costs of production and additionally approximate marginal costs as well. This condition, in which P=MR=MC = Minimum AC, is what ensures least-cost productive efficiency and optimal least price consumer well-being under the pure competitive market model. This ideal condition constitutes the supportive economic justification for the enactment of the antitrust laws and the need to pursue an effective regulatory policy.

MONOPOLISTIC COMPETITION:

Historic and present evidence suggests that this ideal competitive model has never meaningfully dominated the manufacturing sector of the nation's economy. The initial wave of merger activity which commenced around 1880 and the more recent record of acquisitions and firm growth has culminated in structural conditions that are strikingly different from this ideal norm.

While nebulous, the pure competitive model assumes that there is a large number of relatively small-sized firms producing a standardized and very substitutable product. In striking contrast, the monopolistic competitive model is one in which there are a substantially lesser number of firms with the large share of industry activity attributable to a relatively few dominant companies.

The most dominant industry structure within the monopolistic competitive framework is an oligopoly. This type of industrial market structure is characterized by a few large firms. (The Big Three, The Big Four, The Big Eight), accounting for a disproportionate large portion of total market production and sales.[2]

The products being produced within oligopolistic industries may be either standardized or highly differentiated in nature. The products of capital goods producers (steel, aluminum, metals, etc.) are likely to be standardized since the immediate buyer is another firm and not the consuming public. In contrast, consumer goods manufactured for direct retail sale tend to be significantly differentiated with advertising being the principle distributor to the lessened degree of consumer substitutability. This increased consumer allegiance to the product of an individual firm ensures that demand becomes more inelastic, that greater insensitivity to price changes exist, and that the firm has appreciably more discretionary control over pricing. Thus, there is a lessened need for firms to compete on the basis of price. What consumers more typically observe is relatively uniform prices among the firms that increase proportionately over time. This form of oligopolistic industry behavior is summarized in the demand curve illustrated in Fig. 2.

Commonly referred to as a kinked-demand curve, the industry demand function exhibits a relative degree of product elasticity within the range of higher prices or that length of the demand schedule from de to E. Within the range of lower prices, the demand function exhibits a visibly higher degree of product inelasticity as evidenced by the length from E to di:

Fig. 2.

Oligopoly Kinked-Demand Function

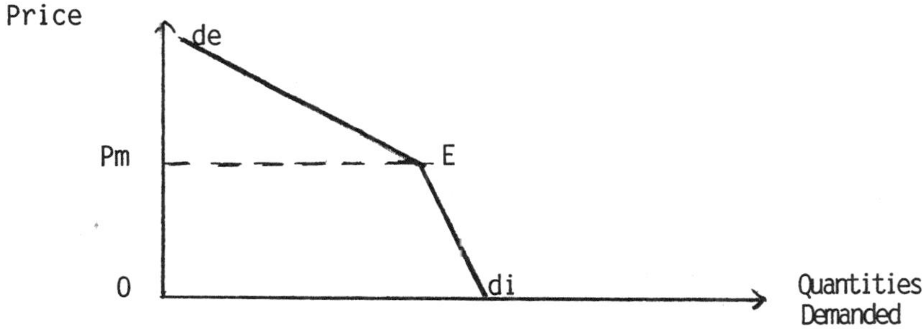

The uniform industry price at which all firms sell their products approximates OPm or that point E on the demand schedule. If any firm within the industry sought to increase its market share by lowering price below the market norm, it would now be confronting the relatively inelastic portion (E-di) of the demand schedule. The lesser price would not appreciably increase firm sales and would likely precipitate price cuts among the remaining firms within the industry. This market behavior would prove to be financially ruinous to all the firms since the price cutting would not measurably increase sales to offset the initial price declines. Thus, consumers are rarely treated to "price wars" and further recognize that such an experience tends to be short-lived.

Alternatively, one firm within the industry is not likely to increase price above the uniform market norm unless there exists the predictable expectation that all other firms will increase their prices to an equal level. Note that within the range of prices above the market price of OPm, the demand schedule (de-E) exhibits relative elasticity. Thus, if a firm increased its product price and maintained it at a level above the uniform industry norm, it would ultimately result in a substantially greater erosion in sales and a net revenue loss. What has been historically exhibited as expected industry behavior is a comparable price increase among all the firms to a higher uniform market level.

This form of market behavior, commonly called price leadership, is a very dominant characteristic of oligopolistic industries. Historically, it had been the largest and most dominant firm which typically initiated the pricing change.

However, some interesting changes have occurred in industry behavior. In some instances, a smaller and less conspicuously dominant firm within the industry has become the first to announce industry wide pricing changes. Commonly called Barometric Price Leadership, all other industry firms would soon announce parallel and uniform pricing changes if no serious adverse market repercussions evolved after the initial firm's announcement.

Regardless of its form, the ultimate result of price leadership is the consistent uniformity of market price among all the firms within the industry. This oligopolistic industry characteristic denies consumers a meaningful choice that might otherwise result from price comparisons among the products of the different industry firms.

TACIT AND OVERT COLLUSION:

The historic and contemporary judicial interpretation of the antitrust laws has critically distinguished between tacit and overt collusion.

Tacit collusion, which most approximates oligopolistic industry behavior, reflects an awareness or recognition among rival firms that forceful price competition would be ruinous to the individual firms and the entire industry. Continued price cutting would not substantially increase sales and ultimately would lead to a rapid and threatening deterioration in revenues and profitability. Thus, while firms do not in a recordable way communicate their interest or willingness to maintain comparable price levels, it is instinctively clear that they must avoid competing among each other on the basis of substantial differences in price. This inferred awareness, without concrete evidence of a conspiracy, is tacit collusion.

Ultimately, the net result and impact of this form of industry behavior is similar to what would occur if the firms had formally, with prior arrangement, overtly agreed to fix prices. In both instances, consumers are denied meaningful differences in price and ultimately elect to purchase a product for other reasons. Overt collusion, which implies a contrived arrangement among competitors to manipulate and distort market conditions is illegal under U.S. antitrust law. Uniformity of selling prices, attributable to a conscious and arranged effort among rival firms to avoid price competition, is a per se violation of law.

In striking contrast, the same market impact, arrived at through an implied awareness (tacit collusion), is not a readily accepted violation of law. This question of inferential conspiracy has been judicially tested on a number of occasions without a definitive interpretation having evolved. While it may not appear to be very competitive when firms pursue parallel pricing behavior, it has not become a consistently interpreted violation without concrete and documentable evidence.

LUMBER DEALERS TRADE ASSOCIATION CASE:

One very early case that involved the question of implied, but undocumented conspiracy, was decided by the Supreme Court in 1914.[3] The court denied the Lumber Dealers Trade Association the authority to provide its member companies with the names of those wholesalers that were retailing directly to customers. The Court's decision centered upon the implied expectation that the member companies would refuse to sell to the wholesalers as a means of eliminating this competitive alternative and thus enhance their mutual market interests. The lack of documented evidence among the firms did not restrain the Court's decision in this case.

AMERICAN TOBACCO COMPANY CASE:

Another case that involved a judicial interpretation of implied and parallel market behavior occurred in 1946. The domestic tobacco industry has and continues to be a very concentrated industry. Dominated by three large companies, American Tobacco, Reynolds, and Ligget and Myers, it has been historically an industry characteristic that the rival firms avoid forceful and direct price competition. In addition to maintaining identical retail prices, the firms had equally bid the same purchase price for tobacco at leaf auctions. This pattern of maintaining identical purchase and retail prices was a historically entrenched form of industry behavior. While the implied and inferential evidence regarding the firm's intentions of avoiding price competition was overwhelmingly complete, there was no documentation or recordable examples of overt collusive behavior. Nevertheless, the Court decreed that the circumstantial and cumulative evidence was sufficient to imply wrongful intent. The court stated:

> "No formal agreement is necessary to constitute an unlawful conspiracy... The essential combination or conspiracy in violation of the Sherman Act may be found in a course of dealings or other circumstances as well as in an exchange of words." [5]

These examples which illustrate effective prosecution of implied oligopolistic tacit collusion are very limited and are not indicative of a consistent judicial interpretation of the antitrust laws. More likely, this behavior which is commonly identified as the "Doctrine of Conscious Parallelism", is interpreted as inadequately circumstantial and permissable under the current interpretation of the law.

THEATER ENTERPRISES v. PARAMOUNT FILM CASE:

A very important case which depicts this more likely judicial view, involved the distribution of first-run movies to theaters in the Baltimore area.[6] The owner of a suburban theater brought suit against nine film distribution companies for their refusal to supply his theater with new movie releases. Instead, the companies released the films exclusively to the downtown city theaters. The suburban theater owner charged that this failure to furnish his business was attributable to a conspiracy which jeopardized his business. During the litigation there was no documented evidence to confirm a willful conspiracy among the film distributors. Rather, the companies defended their similar activity as a prudent business decision because of the greater advertising and increased market potential of a city located theater. The Supreme Court ruled that this was a justifiable and profitable decision on behalf of the distribution companies and could not be construed as a maliciously-inspired conspiratory act. This decision substantially weakened any anticipated enforcement of implied and parallel market behavior among rival industry firms. The Supreme Court stated that:

> "This Court has never held that proof of parallel business behavior...itself constitutes a Sherman Act offense. Circumstantial evidence of consciously parallel behavior may have made heavy inroads into the traditional judicial attitude toward conspiracy; but "conscious parallelism" has not yet read conspiracy out of the Sherman Act entirely." [7]

A more recent example of legal action to effect implied and tacit collusion involved the FTC complaint against the cereal preparations industry.[8] The Federal Trade Commission charged that this highly concentrated industry had sought to avoid meaningful price competition and had relied exclusively upon advertising as the competitive norm among the firms.

In sum, circumstantial evidence that illustrates parallel and identical firm behavior within an industry remains unprosecutable under the present interpretation of the antitrust laws. While the impact upon the consuming public may be equally as injurious as a documented overt collusive agreement, the courts have been generally unwilling to rule against independently evolved, but uniformally practiced, market conditions.

PURE MONOPOLY STRUCTURE:

The extreme market structure that exhibits complete concentration and visible lack of any industry competition is the Pure Monopoly model. It implies the existence of only one firm as the sole producer of the product.

There have been few instances in which firms have successfully achieved a market share that closely approximated a monopoly position within their industry. The most publicized example involved the American Aluminum Co. (ALCOA) which at one point maintained a market share of over 90 percent. This condition was the object of a highly publicized court decision that in essence reaffirmed the illegality of a pure monopoly or closely approximated monopoly position.

The illegality of this type of market structure is evident. One firm, accounting for all industry production and sales, has unbounded manipulative control over the market and seriously jeopardizes the interests of consumers who have no alternative or substitutable product choice. It is the antithesis of a pure competitive market condition and raises serious interpretative questions regarding the optimal functioning of the market process.

THE WASTES OF MONOPOLISTIC COMPETITION:

The striking disparities in output levels, product distribution and market prices that result when products are alternatively produced under Pure Competitive or Monopolistic market conditions is illustrated in Fig. 3.

The pure monopolist seeks to maximize profits and will produce that level of output OQm where MR=MC at point Em. The corresponding market price at that level of output is OPm. In contrast, if the product were being produced under pure competitive conditions, production and selling price would tend to approximate the market condition depicted at Ec where selling price would equal marginal cost and minimum average costs of production. Note that if these market conditions prevailed, the pure competitive market selling price would be OPc and total industry output and sales would be OQc.

Fig. 3.

Wastes of Monopolistic Competition

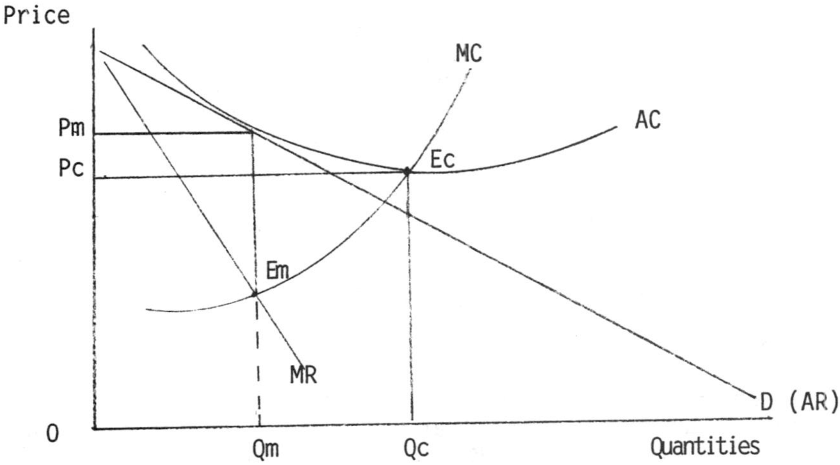

In sum, under a monopoly structure, total production would be appreciably less (OQm) than the total level of output forthcoming from producer activity under a pure competitive condition (OQc). Equally, consumers would pay a substantially higher price (OPm) and consume appreciably less than the selling price determined under a competitive structure (OPe). In addition to the evident differences in production and selling prices is the equally important question regarding market efficiency. Products are not being produced under least cost conditions under the monopoly model whereas the competitive level of output is equated with minimum average costs of production. Thus, under these least cost conditions, it is assumed that resources are being allocated at least-cost into production and that finished goods are being distributed into consumption at least price (Price equals minimum average costs of production).

While the complexities of the market cannot be that simplistically illustrated, it is a useful and real illustration of the differences in market behavior and performance among the different structural models. More importantly, it is the basis upon which economic analysis can supportively justify the need to advance a regulatory policy which strives to preserve a competitive market environment.

SUMMARY:

Competitive industry conditions must exist to ensure the functioning of the capitalistic, market-oriented economy. The pure competitive industry model suggests that product prices are market-determined and that individual firms within the industry do not exert any manipulative influence upon the market. Equally, it is assumed that products will be produced at least-cost and that consumers will pay a price which approximates the minimum costs of production.

In contrast, non-competitive industry conditions suggest that more dominant firm(s) maintain a discretionary influence upon their product markets. The lack of vigorous price competition among the industry firms and the identity of pricing behavior becomes very pronounced within oligopolistic markets.

The supportive justification for antitrust policy is to regulate industry behavior and effect the structural conditions within industries to ensure that competitive markets are preserved.

Footnotes

1. An economic profit exists when P exceeds AC. When price equals AC, the firm incurs a normal profit in which revenue covers both explicit and implicit costs of production. Explicit costs are accountable expenses incurred in the production process while implicit costs are interpretatively an additional return which depict opportunity costs or alternative uses. It's a necessary return (or cost) to justify continued production.

2. Kaysen and Turner categoried oligopolistic industries into either Type I or Type II. A Type I was an oligopoly industry in the eight largest firms accounted for at least 50 but less than 75% of total sales and the twenty largest accounted for at least 75%. A Type II oligopoly consisted of an industry in which the eight largest firms had a market share of 33 but less than 50% and the twenty largest had a share of at least 50% but less than 75%.

3. Eastern States Retail Lumber Dealers Association v. United States, 234 U.kS. 600 (1914).

4. American Tobacco Co., et al., v. U.S., 328 U.S. 781 (1946).

5. Ibid., pp. 809-810.

6. Theater Enterprises, Inc. v. Paramount Firm Distributing Corp. et al., 346 U.S. 537 (1954).

7. Ibid., pp. 809-810.

8. FTC v. Kellogg et., Docket No. 8883 (1972).

CHAPTER READINGS

Greer, Douglas, F. Industrial Organization and Public Policy, Macmillian Publishing Co. Inc. New York, 1980. Chap. 1,2.

Inman, James, E. The Regulatory Environment of Business, John Wiley and Sons., New York, 1984. Chap. 1,2.

Koch, James, V. Industrial Organization and Prices, Prentice-Hall Inc., Englewood Cliffs, New Jersey, 1974, Chap. 2,5,13.

McConnell, Campbell, R., Economics, Principles, Problems, and Policies, Mc-Graw-Hill Book Co., 1981, Chap. 26,27,28,29.

Petersen, Craig, Business and Government, Harper and Row Publishers, New York, 1981, Chap. 2.

CHAPTER TWO

ECONOMIC CONCENTRATION: ITS CAUSES AND EFFECT

The issue of economic concentration and the incidence of monopoly power is of pivotal importance, and meaningfully relates to the very technological, material, and ideological foundation of the nation. It is also a controversial issue that has consumed the attention and interest of countless authorities and congressional committees for decades. Much has been written about the alleged directive and manipulative impact which a select few firms maintain on the nation's economy. Is America a corporate state that responds notably to the interests of big businesses and is driven by the singular obsession to maximize profits and ensure the limited interests of a select segment of the nation's population?

Alternatively, in what ways and by what means has bigness contributed to the continued economic advance of the nation. Has it accelerated the corporate community's support of research and development and ensured the evident flow of new technologies and innovations? Has bigness equally exhibited a social conscience which has partially negated the potentially impersonal and inequitable by-products of the market system?

These questions and many more are an integral part of the debate that centers on monopoly power and corporate bigness in America.

ABSOLUTE AND RELATIVE SIZE CONCENTRATION:

The size of a company can be measured in different ways and may have varied interpretative meaning under the antitrust laws. One standard, called Absolute Size Concentration is a measure of the firm's sales volume, asset size, or number of employees in comparison to other companies. One may reasonably note that Company A with annual sales of many billions is a relatively large-sized firm when compared to Company E whose sales approximate a few million dollars. Equally, Company C employs almost 500,000 workers and is comparatively large-sized when measured against Company D with a total labor force of 500 people.

The annual Fortune Directory of the largest corporations provides an immediate record of those manufacturing firms which would be categorized as big on the basis of absolute size concentration. Manufacturing giants such as Exxon, General Motors, GE, IBM and many others are recognizably large absolute-sized corporations.

This measure of bigness has been and continues to be immune from antitrust prosecution since it does not represent a quantifiable indicator of the individual firm's market share within its industry. Absolute size bigness itself does not confirm a prosecutable illegality under the law.

Table I summarizes the share of manufacturing value-added attributable to various size categories of firms during different years.

Table -1 [1]

Share of Manufacturing Value Added Attributable To:

Firm Size	1972	1967	1963	1958	1954	1947
largest 50 Firms	25	25	25	23	23	17
largest 100 Firms	33	33	33	30	30	23
largest 200 Firms	43	42	41	38	37	30

The evidence confirms the skewed distribution of value-added manufacturing activity within the economy. The largest 50 companies account for 25 percent of all activity and the 100 largest firms are contributing a total of 33 percent. Among the 200 largest, which comprise about one-tenth of one percent of the entire corporate population within the manufacturing sector, the total value of their manufacturing value-added activity comprises 43 percent of the total. The data illustrates the relatively dominant role of the limited few big corporations and confirms the marginal impact of the largest portion of smaller-sized companies. Recognize, however, that there is no concrete information that identifies the relative share of specific industry or market sales that is attributable to any of these big-sized companies. It is a meaningful indicator of the dominant role in total manufacturing activity assumed by these firms and as such is a non-prosecutable measure of absolute-size concentration.

RELATIVE-SIZE CONCENTRATION:

A measure of a firm's shape of total market production or sales within its industry is its relative-size concentration. It identifies that portion of the industry market over which the individual firm or collective group of firms have measurable leverage and control. As such, it is a quantifiable measure of structural conditions within an industry and has been the historical norm used to prosecutably determine an illegality under the antitrust laws.

What market share constitutes an acceptable competitive condition or alternatively is judged as excessively monopolistic, remains the interpretative judgment of the court. At present, there does not exist any steadfast judicial norm and the courts over the years have rendered substantially different and often inconsistent interpretations of illegal monopoly as assessed by relative-size concentration.

A common method of determining relative-size concentration is the use of a concentration ratio.

CONCENTRATION RATIO:

Deriving concentration ratios for individual industries is based upon data which is collected and categorized according to the Standard Industrial Classification system. Statistics which are reported at the two digit level represent divisional and broad industry activity which encompasses the following areas: wholesale trade, retail trade; finance; insurance and real estate; agriculture, forestry and fishing; construction; manufacturing; transportation, communication, electric, gas, and sanitary services; public administration; mining.[2]

TABLE - II [2]

SIC Code System

SIC Code	Designation	Product
20	Major Industry Groupings	Food & Kindred Products
203	Industry Groups	Canning, preserving
2037	Industry & Product Group	Frozen Fruits & vegetables
20371	Product Classification	Frozen Fruits, juices
2037135	Specific Product	Frozen strawberries

While they are a meaningful approximation of structural conditions, it is important to note that concentration ratios do not concisely indicate the actual distribution of firms within the industry. For example, the four-firm concentration ratio for Industry A may be 50 percent in which the largest firm has a market share of 15 percent and the remaining 35 percent is equally divided among the remaining three firms. In contrast, the four-firm concentration ratio for Industry B may also be 50 percent but the dominant firm within this industry might have a market share of 44 percent and the remainder equally divided among the remaining three firms.

The competitive conditions within these two industries is strikingly different with the dominant firm in Industry B having an evident monopolistic market share.

In addition, the concentration ratios are a measure of domestic industry and firm activity and thus exclude the competitive impact of foreign competition within the domestic market. Within many domestic industries, imports constitute a substantial and growing share of total market activity. Thus, the addition of imports may significantly intensify the incidence of actual competitive conditions within a domestic industry. For this reason, it is very important to consider the measured impact of foreign trade when using concentration ratios as a measure of relative-size concentration.

TABLE-III[3]

SIC Code	Industry	Percent of Market Shipments Accounted for By 4 largest firms	8 largest firms
3711	Passenger Cars	99+	100
2834	Pharmaceutical Preparations	24	43
3143	Men's footwear, except athletics	31	46
3621	Motors & Generators	42	55
3312	Steel Mills	45	65
2822	Synthetic Rubber	60	83
3221	Glass Containers	54	75
3724	Aircraft engines	74	86
3632	Household Refrigerators	82	98
2067	Chewing Gum	93	99
2062	Cane Sugar Refining	63	90
2522	Metal Office Furniture	47	59
2631	Paperboard Mills	27	42

The data in Table III suggests that a select few dominant firms, as measured by absolute and relative size standards, have a substantial impact upon the nation's economy. A limited few companies account for a disproportionate share of total manufacturing activity and tend to equally dominant their respective industry markets.

CAUSES OF CONCENTRATION:

The United States has and continues to be notably a nation comprised of small-sized businesses. That is, the largest portion of all incorporated businesses within the manufacturing, retail, and construction sectors tend to be of a relatively small-sized nature.[3] However, the recognizably large-sized firms tend to account for the largest portion of total market and industry activity within all sectors of the economy.

The structural incidence of monopolistic elements within an industry is the result of many different market conditions. Technological and capitalization requirements needed to produce certain types of products may seriously constrain many firms from successfully entering an industry. Additionally, the characteristics of final demand, the growth of the market, and the receptiveness of consumers to other substitutable products within the industry may equally impede the emergence of new firms. In sum, it is barriers to entry which either prohibit or permit the competitive entrance of firms into an industry and determines the structural conditions which exist. This relationship between barriers to entry and structural characteristics is clear. High barriers prevent the emergence of new firms and thus diminish the competitive character and intensity of the industry. Alternatively low barriers to entry suggest a relative ease of entry into the industry and a structurally competitive industry mode.

PRODUCT OF DIFFERENTIATION:

A major cause of unsurmountable high entry barriers is product differentiation. It comprises intangible and equally evident characteristics which lessen consumer substitutability and ensures buyer's allegiance to a specific product. Thus, an individual will insistently buy only Product A regardless of the number of alternative substitutes that may be available on the market and will exhibit an insensitiveness to price differences among the products.

In contrast, standardized products are characterized by a high degree of consumer substitutability and an indifference to product preference. For most consumers, potatoes grown in Maine or Idaho or anywhere else tend to have equal purchase appeal.

Equally while a consumer may seriously deliberate over the purchase of alternative brand-name products, little if any regard is given to what companies produced the steel or aluminum in their fabrication and assembly. Metals, potatoes, and many other products are typically standardized, with little or no consumption preferences exhibited by the consuming public.

Product differentiation results from many varied product related conditions. Actual or perceived differences in product quality, durability, or functional usefulness can contribute to consumer insistance for a specific product. In addition, a meaningful difference in a warranty or guarantee might noticeably influence consumer preference for one product in relation to the others within the market. These types of influences may be very real and tangibly evident to the consumer. Thus, there is a sense of having made a rational and objectively preferred choice based upon quality and price considerations.

ADVERTISING AND PRODUCT DIFFERENTIATION:

A noted contributor to consumer preferences based on product differentiation is advertising as this often persuasively impacts upon consumer behavior. Advertising may informatively relate physical differences among products and thus enable a consumer to ultimately make a better and more "educated" choice. Beyond its informative value, advertising tends to additionally effect consumption behavior because of its persuasive and brand identification impact. Once consumers identify with a brand-name product, they increasingly refrain from purchasing alternatives and exhibit an insensitiveness to differences in market prices.

Advertising has become the primary form of direct non-price competition among firms within monopolistic competitive industries. It represents a substantial cost outlay for individual firms that is ultimately reflected in the product's selling price.

Total advertising expenditures in 1984 among the nation's 100 largest advertisers approximated $18.4 bill and the advertising to sales ratio averaged 2.9 percent. Of the total, $11.7 bill was spent on measured media, such as television, radio, newspapers, and magazines.[5] An additional $7.2 bill was spent by these firms on so-called unmeasured advertising, which includes direct mail, trade show promotions, and transit type visual messages.[6]

Table IV presents statistical information on total advertising expenditures among the nation's leading advertisers. The industry advertising to sales ratio was highest among pharmaceutical manufacturers (13.8%) and is followed by the cosmetics industry (12.4%), and the soap and detergent industry (10.2%). While this ratio varies appreciably among individual firms within these industries, it is interesting to note that it is highest among the select few dominant firms. This confirms the important use of advertising as a non-price competitive norm within the oligopolistic industry setting.

Effective advertising, which reduces the degree of product substitutability, will contribute to greater elasticity of market demand and provide the producing firm with increased discretionary control over product price. As firms seek to maximize their revenue flows, they are able to effectively increase product price without seriously eroding their product's sales base. Thus unwavering allegiance to an advertised brand-name product and the insensitivity which consumers then exhibit to upward changes in its product price is the firm's advertising objective.

TABLE-IV [7]

Advertising Expenditures Among Select Firms (1984)

Company	Advertising Expenditures	Adv./Sales Ratio
Proctor & Gamble	773,618,300	(8.1%)
Sears, Roebuck Co.	732,500,000	(2.2)
General Motors Co.	595,129,500	(0.9%)
R.J. Reynolds	593,350, 300	(5.5)
Philip Morris Inc.	527,481,800	5.7
Ford Motor Co.	479,060,000	1.5
A T & T	463,095,500	0.7
K Mart Corp.	400,000,000	2.2
General Foods Corp.	386,134,200	6.0
Nabisco Brands	367,530,400	10.1
Pepsi Co. Inc.	356,400,000	5.3
Warner-Lambert Co.	343,553,500	18.9
American Home Products, Inc.	333,485,000	9.6
Unilever U.S.	324,865,800	12.2
McDonald's Corp.	311,378,000	4.0
Johnson & Johnson	295,328,800	8.2
Mobil Corp.	294,932,500	1.2
Anheuser-Bush Co.	290,616,400	4.4
Ralston-Purina Co.	285,667,400	7.4
Coca-Cola Co.	282,150,000	6.9
General Mills	268,690,200	5.3
Colgate-Palmolive Co.	268,000,000	12.2
Bristol-Myers Co.	235,000,000	8.1
Chrysler Corp.	230,020,100	2.0
RCA Corp.	212,300,000	2.7
Dart & Kraft	210,279,400	3.0
H.J. Heinz Co.	202,400,000	7.9

TABLE IV Continued

Company	Advertising Expenditures	Adv./Sales Ratio
G.E.	196,506,000	1.1
Consolidated Foods	195,858,000	3.0
Pillsbury Co.	190,944,300	4.6
Gillette Co.	185,604,400	18.2
Mattel Inc.	179,943,800	21.4
Kellogg Co.	176,306,900	11.3
Sterling Drug	171,828,100	24.4
Tandy Corp.	156,728,000	6.7
Quaker Oats, Inc.	148,441,700	9.1
Campbell Soaps	126,000,000	4.6
Richardson-Vicks	150,813,900	22.6
IBM	119,222,500	0.5
Nestle Enterprises	114,957,000	4.6
Revlon	123,968,900	7.5
Strob Brewery Co.	73,532,400	4.7
Hershey Foods Corp.	68,257,400	4.0
Wendy's International	64,445,000	3.4
Wm. Wrigley Jr. Co.	63,948,200	15.7

DEMAND ELASTICITY: PRICE CHANGES AND REVENUE FLOWS:

This firm objective is represented in the relationship between demand elasticity, changes in product price, and the resulting impact upon revenue flows.

Elasticity of demand is a measure of how consumers will respond to a change in product price. It is calculated as the percentage change in quantity demanded that results from (or is divided by) the percentage change in the product's selling price.

$$\text{Demand Elasticity (Ed)} = \frac{\text{Percentage change in quantity demanded}}{\text{Percentage change in Price}}$$

$$Ed = \frac{dQ}{Q} \div \frac{dP}{P}$$

To illustrate, let us assume the following price and quantity demand relationship. At a price of 20 dollars each, 20 units of the product have been sold. The selling price then declined to 15 dollars and the consumer then purchased 30 units. To calculate the elasticity of demand for the product:

$$E_d = \frac{10}{20} \div \frac{-5}{20} = \frac{1}{2} \times \frac{4}{-1} = \frac{4}{-2} = -2$$

The calculated demand elasticity is Ed = 2. There is always a negative sign in the calculation because of the inverse relationship between price changes and quantity demanded as expressed in the Law of Demand.

The numerical value of the coefficient, 2, indicates that the inverse change in quantity demanded, or the firm's sales, will be twice that of the initial change in price. Thus, if price decreased by 5 percent, quantity demanded will increased by 10 percent.

It is important to note that a numerical coefficient greater than 1 suggests that demand is elastic in nature; that consumers are very responsive to a price change or that the percentage change in quantity demanded will exceed the percentage change in price.

A numerical coefficient of less than 1 suggests that demand is inelastic in nature; that consumers are not very responsive to a price change, and that the percentage change in quantity demanded will be less than the initial percentage change in price.

This has very important pricing and revenue implications to a firm. When demand is elastic, a price change for the product results in an inverse change in the firm's revenue flows. As in our example, when Ed = 2; if a firm increased price by 10 percent, it is expected that quantity demand (sales) will decrease by 20 percent and that total revenue received by the firm will decrease.

In striking contrast, an inelastic demand ensures that revenue flows will change directly to changes in product price. If Ed = 1/2, and the firm increased price by 10 percent, then quantity demanded (sales) will decrease by only 5 percent and total revenue flows to the firm will increase.

It is this direct relationship between demand inelasticity, price changes, and the resulting direct impact upon revenue flows that is crucial to the advertising decision. Effective advertising that successfully differentiates a product and lessens the degree of product substitutability contributes to inelasticity of demand. This consumer insensitivity to price changes is what ensures that product prices will rise as firms seek to increase their revenue and potential profitability.

BARRIERS TO ENTRY:

One very important effect of advertising is the evolution of unsurmountably high barriers-to-entry which erodes the incidence of structurally competitive market conditions. This situation is illustrated in Fig. II.

Fig. II

Economy-To-Scale Barrier to Entry

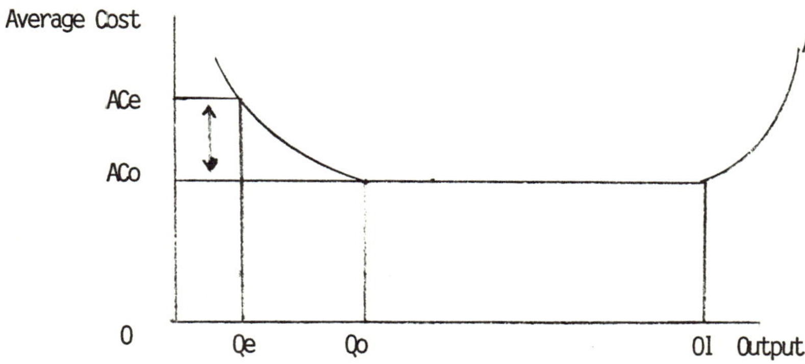

The dominant and established firms within the industry are producing within the range of OQo and OQ1. Note that within this range of output, production costs are uniformally the same, OACo, for all of the established firms. The new entering firm is able to produce and sell the amount OQe. Note that the new firm's average cost will be substantially higher than that of the dominant and established firms. It will incur average costs of OACe.

In general, unless a new firm is able to minimally produce at least OQo or achieve that level of market penetration within an established industry, it will not competitively survive. This type of scale barrier to entry is very real and a major contributor to non-competitive structural conditions within the economy. Estimates of the minimum share of the national market needed within different industries to achieve a least-cost economy to scale position are contained in Table V.

TABLE-V [8]

Minimum Efficient Scale Plants (1967)

Industry	Percent of National Output
Turbogenerators	23.0
Refrigerators	13.0
Homemade Laundry Equip.	11.2
Manmade Fiber	11.1
Aircraft (Commercial)	10.0
Synthetic Rubber	7.2
Cigarettes	6.6
Transformers	4.9
Paperboard	4.4
Tires and Inner Tubes	3.8
Blast Furnaces and Steel	2.7
Detergents	2.4
Petroleum refining	1.8
Paints and varnishes	1.4
Beer	1.1
Shoes	0.2
Four Mills	0.7
Machine Tools	0.3
Cotton Textiles	0.2

While incomplete, the representative data suggest that economy-to-scale considerations do not justify the need for dominant firm concentration within most industries. Indeed, the evidence strongly suggest that most industries, (including those with atypically high capitalization requirements, Aircraft, Transformers, Steel, Petroleum-refining, etc.) could competitively sustain a much larger number of producing firms. While this conclusion must be tempered because of geographic market considerations and multiplant economies, one may reasonably conclude that economy-to-scale considerations pose only a moderate barrier to entry within most domestic industries. In reality, however, it is the impact of the advertising and the resulting differentiation that contributes to these excessively high economy-to-scale barriers rather than least-cost considerations.

Striking differences in absolute costs may pose an additional impediment to the successful emergence of a new firm within an industry. For varied reasons, including technological and financial considerations, a new firm may experience higher production costs at all levels of output than those incurred by established companies. Fig. III illustrates this condition.

Fig. III

Absolute Cost Barrier-To-Entry

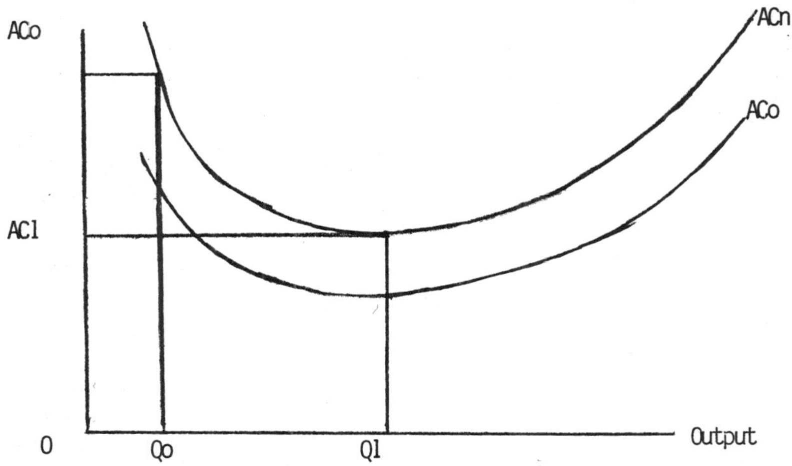

The average cost function of producing at varied output levels for the established firms is summaried in OACo. In contrast, the cost of producing at different output levels for the new emerging firms is depicted in ACn. It is evident that the new firm will be unable to be cost competitive at any level of output and will beforced to withdraw from the industry.

This cost disadvantage might represent the substantially higher interest charges on the serviceable debt of the entering firm. Equally, the established firms may have successfully monopolized the industry's relevant patents which would place the emerging firm at a technological-cost disadvantage. Additionally, the cost disparity might represent the exorbitant advertising expenses which the new firm has incurred in striving to promote its product within the industry market.

Interestingly, it is this latter consideration that has been advanced as an argument in support of advertising as a contributor to intensified competition within an industry.

In referring again to Fig. III, let us assume that the new firm's initial market share is represented by the output level OQo. In producing this quantity, the new firm's average costs approximates OACo which may be substantially higher than the costs experienced by the established companies. Thus, the emerging company, in striving to ensure its successful market penetration, spends substantial sums on advertising promotion. The immediate effect of this promotional effort may further widen its absolute cost disadvantage, but may ultimately prove beneficial if it successfully expands the firm's sales and production level to OQ1. Note that at this higher output level the firm's average production costs have declined from ACo to AC1. Thus, whole absolute production costs are initially higher, the entering firm's unit costs are less and its competitive survival has been substantially enhanced.

This could be very strong support in defense of advertising as a major contributor to the creation of structurally competitive market conditions. However, overwhelming evidence has confirmed the strong positive correlation between advertising, product differentiation, the erection of prohibitively high barriers-to-entry and the existence of monopolistic market structures.

Ironically, government policy has not always contributed to the preservation of competitive market structures. Rather, through the enactment of contradictory legislation, the issuance of directives and regulatory guidelines, and changes in the vigor with which potential violations are prosecuted, public policy has often been an added cause of economic concentration within the economy. An examination of the monopolistic implications of inconsistent public policy is discussed in a later chapter.

MARKET CONDUCT AND INDUSTRY PERFORMANCE:

The relationships between the structural characteristics of an industry and the resulting nature of firm behavior and industry conduct has been exhaustively reviewed. As earlier noted, there is the very real expectation that production and pricing levels should be substantially different among either atomistically competitive or monopolistic markets. In sum, prices are expectedly higher when products are manufactured under increasingly monopolistic conditions. It implies very serious interpretive questions about the efficiency with which resources are allocated into production of goods and services for the well-being of the consuming public.

In addressing this issue it is important to examine the relationships between economic concentration, the existence of market power within the industry, and the profit performance of the firms. Very conclusively, most studies have demonstrated a positive and very strong correlation between industry concentration levels, market power, pricing strategy, and profit performance.[10]

Productive and distributive cost economies, the rate of market growth, and many other considerations importantly affect the profitability of a firm or an entire industry. It is clear, however, that a major determinant is the structural characteristics of the industry and the direct leverage and control which a firm or select dominant firms have over their product markets.

The correlated relationship between industry concentration, market power, and profitability raises a very critical policy issue that was observed during the depression of the 30's.[11] Gardiner Means and others observed that prices among products identified with concentrated industries not only failed to decline but in some cases increased in spite of the sharp and substantial decreases in market demand. They suggested that this inflexibleness of price and its failure to respond to market changes was attributed to administered pricing policies among dominant firms within monopolistic industries.

The administered pricing thesis assumes that firms with sufficient market control and power will set or administer a price to ensure a targeted corporate objective-such as an expected rate of return. Thus, a decrease in product demand will prompt a firm to maintain or more notably raise product price as a means of insulating itself from the lessened sales volume.

This market condition may seriously erode the effectiveness of both fiscal and monetary policy measures used to effect the direction of the nation's economy. Targeted pricing might actually heighten inflationary pressures since successful policy efforts to reduce aggregate demand and alleviate inflation might prompt administered increases in product prices.

Equally such a market condition seriously undermines the operativeness of the market, negates the directive role of the consuming public, and erodes the ideological foundation of the nation's capitalist economic system.

SUMMARY:

While the nation consists of a large number of businesses, it is notably a few, large-sized companies within concentrated industries which tend to dominate the nation's economy.

Various conditions contribute to the erection of unsurmountable barriers-to-entry which in turn affects the incidence of monopolistic elements within an industry. High barriers-to-entry lessens industry competition which in turn heightens the incidence of monopolistic dominance upon product prices and overall consumer choice. It is these forms of market imperfections that regulatory policy seeks to correct.

FOOTNOTES

1. Dept. of Commerce, Concentration Ratios in Manufacturing: 1972 Census of Manufacturing (Washington, D.C. U.S. Gov. Printing Office), 1975.

2. Standard Industrial Classification Manual, (Washington, D.C.) Government Printing Office, 1972.

3. U.S. Bureau of the Census, Census of Manufacturers, 1977, Concentration Ratios in Manufacturing, MC 77-SR-9, Washington, D.C. 1981.

4. Advertising Age, Crain Communications Co., N.Y., N.Y., pg. 8. Sept. 14, 1984.

5. Ibid., pg. 8

6. Ibid., pg. 8

7. Advertising Age, Crain Communications Co., N.Y., N.Y., Sept. 14, 1984, pag. 8

8. D.F. Green, Industrial Organization & Public Policy, 2nd ed. Macmillan Publishing Co. N.Y., 1984, p. 165.

9. Ibid, pp. 166-169

10. A credible review of this relationship can be found in: Leonard W. Weiss, "The Concentration-Profits Relationship" in Industrial Concentration: the New Learning, edited by H. Godschmid, M. Mann, and F. Weston, Little, Brown, (Boston, Ma.) 1974, pp. 196-201, J.A. Dalton and D.W. Penn, The Quality of Data as a Factor in Analysis of Structure-Performance Relationships (FTC Report), 1971., A Rhoades and J.M. Cleaver, "The Nature of the Concentration-Price/Cost Margin Relationship for 352 Manufacturing Industries: 1967" Southern Economic Journal, July, 1973, pp. 90-102.

11. Gardiner C. Means, The Corporate Revolution In America, Cronwell-Collier, New York, 1962. pp. 77-96

CHAPTER READINGS

Blair, John, M. Economic Concentration: Structure, Behavior, and Public Policy, Harcourt Brace Jovanovich, Inc. New York, 1972, Chap. 1,2,3,4

Greer, Douglas, F. Industrial Organization and Public Policy, MacMillan Publishing Co., New York, 1980. Chap. 2,3.

Koch, James, V. Industrial Organization and Prices, Prentice-Hall, Inc. Englewood Cliffs, New Jersey, 1974, Chap. 4,6,7,8.

Means, Gardiner, C. The Corporate Revolution in America, Cromwell-Collier, New York, 1962.

Shcerer, Frederic, M. Industrial Market Structure and Economic Performance, Rand McNally and Co., Chicago, 1970. Chap. 2,4,8,14.

CHAPTER THREE

THE ANTITRUST LAWS AND ENFORCEMENT

The early legislative initiative for the antitrust laws was attributable to the widespread and evident abuses that accompanied rapid economic growth after the Civil War. The period of rapid industrialization which began in the 1870's witnessed an unprecedented wave of mergers and the formation of business trusts that dramatically altered the structural characteristics of the nation's economy. Consolidations among competing firms went unchallenged and contributed to singular monopolistic dominance within several industries.

The trust arrangement resulted in independent and competing firms being placed under a common ownership and control. They were formed when majority stockholders of different companies assigned their ownership shares to a single group of trustees. As compensation, the stockholders received trust certificates which entitled them to participate in the profitability of the newly formed trust which operated as a single entity. This legal arrangement consolidated formerly competitive rival firms into a dominant monopolistic force within an industry and was a major contributor to the rise of economic concentration during this period.

Without serious fear of prosecution, various predatory abuses evolved which jeopardized the competitive survival of many smaller sized firms and further entrenched the monopolistic position of the dominant firms.

It became increasingly evident that more specific and restraining legislation was needed to supplement the inadequacies of the earlier used common law precedents. This recognized need for a national government response became a leading issue of the presidential election in 1888. Following much debate and compromise revisions, the nation's first antitrust law was legislated in 1890.

THE SHERMAN ANTITRUST ACT OF 1890:

Named after one of its chief advocates, Senator John Sherman of Ohio, the Sherman Act sought to address the critical issues of established monopoly power and the various types of anti-competitive behavior that contributed to the monopolization of domestic markets. The first legislated antitrust statute, the law remains the cornerstone of our nation's regulatory policy. It decrees that:

> Sec. 1 Every contract, combination in the form of trust or otherwise, or conspiracy, in restraint of trade or commerce among the several States, or with foreign nations is hereby declared to be illegal. Every person who shall make any such contract or engage in any such combination or conspiracy, shall be deemed guilty of a misdemeanor, and, on conviction thereof, shall be punished by fine not exceeding five thousand dollars, or by imprisonment not exceeding one year, or by both said punishments, in the discretion of the court.
>
> Sec. 2 Every person who shall monopolize or attempt to monopolize, or combine or conspire with any other person or persons, to monopolize any part of the trade or commerce among the several states, or with foreign nations, shall be deemed guilty of a misdemeanor, and, on conviction thereof, shall be punished by fine not exceeding one year, or by both said punishments in the discretion of the court.

Sec. 1 declares illegal those types of activities or business practices which restrains trade among competitors and ultimately reduces competition within the market. It emphasizes and attacks abusive and predatory conduct among sellers that would jeopardize the competitive survival of rival firms and the well-being of the consumer. But what legally constitutes restraint of trade and what type of specific acts and practices are in violation of the law? The answers to these questions are not defined, are nebulously stated, and have been decided through the interpretative judgment of the courts. Thus, for many years, until after there evolved a consistent judicial interpretation, the thrust of the Sec. 1 provision was weakened by its nonpreventive enforcement. Predatory practices such as price-fixing and marketsharing agreements among firms are presently viewed as per se violations of the law because the courts have rather consistently ruled them to be illegal.

Sec. 2 is directed towards the illegal process of monopolizing trade and commerce and addresses the structural and behavioral issue of monopoly. Much like the ambiguity contained in Sec. 1, this language fails to adequately define what constitutes an illegality. What is an illegal monopoly position? Ultimately these definitional considerations have been interpretatively decided by the courts. In the process of judicial deliberation, the courts have not always been definitionally consistent; emphasizing conduct and behavior as a pivotal norm and later stressing structural characteristics in arriving at a definition of illegal monopoly.

A review of judicial decisions will be introduced in a later chapter but it is interesting to immediately consider an early decision rendered by the Supreme Court. In 1895, the Supreme Court ruled that the E.C. Knight Co., a sugar-refining trust, was not in violation of the Sec. 2 provision of the Sherman Act since the law applied only to commerce and was not intended to regulate manufacturing activity.[1]

INTERSTATE AND INTRASTATE COMMERCE:

It is important to note that this statute and all Federal regulatory legislation jurisdictionally applies to interstate and foreign commerce. Interstate commerce is business activity that extends beyond the territorial bounds of one state. A firm that produces and/or distributes products within the national market, a regional market, or is limited to two states is subject to federal antitrust enforcement. In contrast, intrastate commerce is business activity that is contained within the territorial bounds of one state. Such a firm is not directly subject to federal antitrust enforcement but is responsible to the regulatory codes of the individual state within which it is located and engaged in business. Equally, domestic firms engaged in foreign commerce are subject to federal regulatory statutes as are foreign nationals that are engaged in commercial activities within the domestic market.

It is important to note that private parties may bring suit against one another under the provisions of the Sherman Act and be granted financial restitution that may approximate three times the the value of the estimated injury. This type of financial award is referred to as treble damages. More recently, Congress enacted the Antitrust Improvements Act in 1976, which permits the attorney general or individual states to bring suit on behalf of the state residents to collect treble damages in cases of proven injury.

For many reasons, the Sherman Act did not prove to be immediately effective. Its nebulous language and failure to specify definable types of practices and acts which would contribute to illegal restraint of trade eroded its preventive thrust. Additionally, there was an initial hesitancy to forcefully prosecute dominant trusts and big mergers since a definitive and consistent judicial interpretation of illegal monopoly had not been resolved. This early inconsistency, as dramatized in the E.C. Knight case, is representative of the initial ineffectiveness of the law. It then became evident that additional legislation was needed to strengthen the regulatory intent embodied in the Sherman Act by declaring certain types of practices and/or acts to be illegal and to prosecute those conditions which might contribute to monopoly power prior to its actual evolved state.

THE CLAYTON ACT:

The passage of the Clayton Act in 1914 represented a Congressional effort to strengthen the preventive thrust of the nation's regulatory policy. Its main provisions are contained in:

> Sec. 2 It shall be unlawful for any person engaged in commerce to discriminate in price between different purchasers of commodities, ...where the effect of such discrimination may be to substantially lessen competition or tend to create a monopoly in any line of commerce....
>
> Sec. 3 It shall be unlawful for any person engaged in commerce, to lease or make a sale or contract for sale of goods...on the condition, agreement, or understanding that the lessee or purchaser thereof shall not use or deal in the goods...of a competitor or competitors of the lessor or seller, where the effect of such lease sale or contract...may be to substantially lessen competition or tend to create a monopoly in any line of commerce.
>
> Sec. 7 No corporation engaged in commerce shall acquire, directly or indirectly, the whole or any part of the stock or other share capital of another corporation engaged also in commerce where the effect of such acquisition may be to substantially lessen competition between the corporation whose stock is so acquired and the corporation making the acquisition or to restrain such commerce in any section or community or tend to create a monopoly of any line of commerce.

Prior to the passage of the Clayton Act, price discrimination was a rather common predatory, anti-competitive practice. Sellers would enter new markets and offer their product at an unprofitably low level as a means of eliminating existing competition. Once competitors had withdrawn from the market, the firm would then charge an excessive monopolist price in order to subsidize their price-cutting penetration of other new markets. Thus, charging different customers (markets) different prices was an abusive distribution policy that was used to monopolize new markets or maintain an entrenched monopoly position within established markets.

Sec. 2 declares that different customers may be charged different prices only if there are: (1) differences in the quantities purchased (quantity discounts are permissable); (2) substantive differences in the quality of the products purchased by the different consumers (quality differences imply that the products are substantatively different in function or durability, etc.); (3) justifiable and incurred differences in transportation or distribution costs.

This provision was later amended by the enactment of the Robinson-Patman Act in 1936, to regulate the terms of purchase and promotional concessions granted to buyers (notably retailers) to ensure the competitive survival of small retail businesses. This provision, like that of Sec. 3, seeks to prosecute specific types of business behavior which would provingly result in restraint of trade and contribute to the monopolization of domestic markets.

Sec. 3 forbids a seller to obligate a buyer to purchase exclusively from their business since such a prohibitive practice would seriously impede the competitive position of rival firms within the market. Specifically, it addresses two forms of illegal exclusionary practices.

(1) It forbids Tying Contracts in which a seller agrees to the sale of its product only if the buyer additionally agrees to buy other products from it as well. If a business agrees to buy and retail a company's pasta making machine, it is illegal to equally obligate the firm to buy the seller's spaghetti sauce and cheese.

(2) Exclusive-Dealer arrangements are also illegal under this provision. A seller cannot obligate a buyer as a condition of a sale to forego or exclude the sale of its competitor's products since this practice would diminish competition and promote a monopoly condition. A manufacturer of men's apparel cannot obligate a prospective buyer, as a condition of sale, to sell only its line of dress pants, shirts, and ties and exclude from selling the comparable products of its competitors.

These forms of restrictive practices are illegal if they erode the competitive position of competitors and contribute to a monopoly position.

Sec. 7 provision of the Clayton Act deals with mergers and corporate acquisitions that are consummated through the purchase of stock. This serious short-coming was remedied in 1950 with the passage of the Celler-Kefauver Act which decreed that mergers consummated through asset acquisition are illegal if they provingly contribute to monopoly conditions within an industry.

THE FEDERAL TRADE COMMISSION ACT:

The Federal Trade Commission Act, legislated in 1914, created the Federal Trade Commission (FTC). It is a regulatory agency empowered to initiate investigations regarding the structural conditions and behavioral performance of domestic industries. The law further decreed that "unfair methods of competition in commerce are hereby declared unlawful" and permits the Commission to issue "cease and desist orders" to firm(s) if a questioned "unfair" business practice has been introduced.

The enforcement authority of the FTC was strengthened in 1938 when Congress enacted the Wheeler-Lea Act. This amendment injects "unfair or deceptive acts or practices in commerce" as additional forms of business behavior that come under the watchful scrutiny of the FTC as possibly illegal. The Wheeler-Lea Act's passage was precipitated by a lengthy and shocking court case involving the credibility of an advertised remedy for obesity.[2] It was evident that the manufacturer had fraudulently misadvertised the benefits of its product to the consuming public. Yet, there was no legislative precedent to adequately protect the public from this form of business abuse. Thus, the FTC has now assumed the responsibility to scrutinize advertising as a potential "deceptive act or practice in commerce" and to bring appropriate legal action when necessary.

CELLER-KEFAUVER ACT:

The Celler-Kefauver Act of 1950 amended the Sec. 7 provision of the Clayton Act to decree:

> That no corporation engaged in commerce shall acquire, directly or indirectly, the whole or any part of the stock or other share capital and no corporation subject to the jurisdiction of the Federal Trade Commission shall acquire the whole or any part of the assets of another corporation engaged also in commerce where in any line of commerce in any section of the country, the effect of such acquisition may be substantially to lessen competition, or tend to create a monopoly.

This legislation attempted to effectively correct the evident loophole contained in the Sec. 7 anti-merger provision of the Clayton Act. Now, all mergers, consummated through stock or asset acquisition which provingly contribute to a monopoly position or substantially lessen competition are potentially illegal. It was additionally assumed that the added language "in any line of commerce in any section of the country" would significantly strengthen the regulatory officials' efforts to constrain future merger activity. The expectation was that this revised language would effectively block proposed consolidations among suppliers and manufacturers (vertical mergers), rather than just direct competitive rivals (horizontal mergers). Additionally, it was anticipated that mergers among firms producing unrelated products (conglomerate mergers) might be equally blocked under this revision.

The revision additionally accentuates the need to evaluate the impact of a merger within a definable territorial market. Consolidation may not be interpretatively decreed illegal only because they impact monopolistically upon the national market. Rather, the geographical bounds within which a merger may impact can be more narrowly defined to comprise a definable section or regional market. It was assumed that these new interpretative guidelines would significantly strengthen the effective prosecution of questionable merger activity.

INTERPRETATION AND ENFORCEMENT OF ANTITRUST STATUTES:

Antitrust litigation can be initiated through different agencies and parties. Most frequently, the Antitrust Division of the Department of Justice, acting from a received complaint or from information based upon an investigation, will bring suit against a defendant(s). The legal action will be first reviewed by a federal district court and upon appeal may be eventually tried by a circuit court of appeals and the Supreme Court of the United States. Many cases, upon continued appeal, have been ultimately decided by the Supreme Court.

The FTC, when deemed appropriate, may issue a formal complaint that is reviewed by a Commission administrative law judge. If the decision is appealed, the case may then be reviewed by the panel of FTC Commissioners and may then proceed to the federal court system.

Litigation may also be initiated by individual state attorney generals. If the questioned business practice is contained within the state (intrastate commerce), the case would be ajudicated under the individual state's antitrust laws which emulate the federal standards. Additionally, the states' attorney generals are permitted to initiate legal action involving interstate commerce under the provisions of the Antitrust Improvements Act, which was legislated in 1976.

Lastly, legal action can also be introduced on behalf of private parties. A person, persons, or an individual company may file for litigation within the federal courts involving an alleged violation of the antitrust laws.

Over the years, thousands of cases involving violations of the antitrust laws have been reviewed and litigated. We will review a representative sample to illustrate the evolved judicial interpretation of the various provisions of the laws that center upon the issue of monopoly, restraint of trade practices, and mergers.

MONOPOLY: STANDARD OIL OF NEW JERSEY CASE:

A landmark judicial decision which centered upon the question of monopolization occurred in 1911. The Justice Department brought legal proceedings against the John D. Rockefeller owned Standard Oil of New Jersey Co. and charged that the firm had successfully sought to monopolize and restrain trade in crude oil, refined oil, and other petroleum products.[3] Among the alleged violations, it was noted that the company had acquired an excessive 85% to 90% market share of the nations' refined oil sales, that it had extracted preferential rates and rebates from the railroads which were not equally available to its competitors, and that it had engaged in abusive price discrimination within different markets as a means of eliminating existing competition.

The Justice Department requested the court to apply a per se decision involving Sec. 1 of the Sherman Act in which all contracts or combinations in restraint of trade would be readily decreed as illegal. However, the Supreme Court held not all contracts or combinations in restraint of trade were to be judge illegal; rather only evidence of predatory and unreasonable activities were to be condemned. In this decision, the court advanced the "Rule of Reason Doctrine" as an interpretative definition of monopoly under the Sherman Act. The judicial decision stated:

> "In substance the propositions urged by the government are reducible to this: That the language of the statute embraces every contract combination, etc...., in restraint of trade, hence its text leaves no room for the exercise of judgment, but simply imposes the plain duty of applying its prohibitions to every case within its literal language...the construction which we have deduced from the history of this Act and the analysis of its text is simply that in every case where it is claimed that an act or acts are in violation of the statute the rate of reason, in light of the principles of law and the public policy which the Act embodies, must be applied."[4]

In involving the Rule of Reason interpretation, the Court found that this company had advanced and entrenched its monopolistic control of the market with the use of illegal anti-competitive practices. Judged in violation of the Sherman Act, the Supreme Court ordered the Standard Oil of New Jersey Company to be dissolved into thirty-four different companies.

Under the Rule of Reason Doctrine, the court negated the importance of structural characteristics as an interpretative norm. The relative size of the firm, its share of the market or singular industry dominance, is not of pivotal consideration in determining an illegality under the law. Rather, behavioral characteristics and ultimately an evaluation of the firm's market performance becomes the critical determinant in assessing legal or illegal monopoly. In sum a good monopoly is permissable; only a bad monopoly--a firm that abuses its monopoly position or achieves it through predatory and abusive behavior--is to be condemned.

AMERICAN TOBACCO COMPANY CASE:

The Rule of Reason interpretation was again applied in 1911 when the antitrust authorities brought suit against the American Tobacco Company. The Company was charged with having acquired excess monopoly power and the use of abusive, anti-competitive practices. Specifically, a trust was formed in 1890 to include five cigarette manufacturers which extended its market coverage with the purchase of an additional five manufacturers of chewing tobacco in 1898. In addition to having acquired a monopolized hold on its industry markets, the evidence confirmed that the trust engaged in predatory price cutting and other abusive practices to eliminate competition. Thus, the critical determination of the Court was that the firm had achieved and entrenched its monopolistic market position through illegal and anti-competitive behavior. The court reaffirmed the Rule of Reason interpretation of the Sherman Act and ordered the company to be dissolved into fourteen separate corporations.

The Rule of Reason interpretation was effectively used in these two instances and ultimately served to advance the regulatory intent of the Sherman Act. However, in those instances in which there was not sufficient or substantial evidence of behavioral abuse, monopoly power or bigness itself was not to be used as a prosecutable norm. Under these conditions, the Sherman Act became ineffective in preserving structurally competitive conditions within the economy.

U.S. STEEL CORPORATION CASE:

An example of this occurred in 1912, when the Justice Department charged the U.S. Steel Corp. with a Sec. 2 violation of the Sherman Act for maintaining a 50 percent share of iron and steel production.[6] The Company's market share had been achieved through the earlier acquisition of a large number of smaller independent firms which U.S. Steel argued was necessary to ensure adequate vertical integration as well as individual plant specialization. Additionally, the company argued that its size was necessary to achieve manufacturing economies that would enhance its ability to competitively penetrate foreign markets. In applying the Rule of Reason Doctrine, the Supreme Court ruled in 1920 in favor of the company, noting that there was not any confirming evidence that the firm had ever abused its dominant market position. An earlier contention advanced by the government that the firm had engaged in price-fixing activity with its competitors was rejected by the Court. While undeniably a large dominant firm within its industry, but without evidence of abusive and anti-competitive behavior, the Court stated:

> "We have pointed out that there are several of the government's contentions which are difficult to represent or measure, and the one we are now considering--that is, that power is 'unlawful regardless of its purpose', is another of them. It seems to us that it has for its ultimate principle and justification that strength in any producer or seller is a menace to the public interest and illegal, because there is potency in it for mischief ...The Corporation is undoubtably of impressive size, and it takes an effort of resolution not to be afected by it or to exaggerate its influence. But we must adhere to the law, and the law does not make mere size an offense, or the existence of unexerted power an offense. It, we repeat, requires overt acts, and trusts to its prohibition of them and its power to repress or punish them." [7]

Of lesser importance in the Court's decision was the further awareness that U.S. Steel's dominance within the industry had declined during the ten years ending in 1911. The company's share of total industry sales declined from 50.1 to 40.9 percent as other steel manufacturers assumed greater prominence within the industry.

This judicial emphasis upon market conduct and behavior to the disregard of structural characteristics was again reaffirmed in 1916. The regulatory officials brought suit against the American

Can Company charging a violation of Sec. 2 of the Sherman Act.[8] Even though the company had a 90 percent share of tin can production, the Court ruled that it was not in violation of the law since there was no evidence of abusive market behavior which constrained the performance of its competitors.

<u>ALCOA CASE</u>:

This judicial emphasis upon conduct and behavior as the principal evaluative norms to determine monopoly under Sec. 2 of the Sherman Act continued until 1945. In that year, the regulatory officials charged ALCOA with having successfully monopolized the following markets: alumina, virgin aluminum, castings, pistons, bauxite, cooking utensils, foil, sheet and cable; or in sum the manufacture of virgin aluminum and the distribution of various aluminum products.[9]

The case was initially adjudicated in a federal district court which dismissed the charges and found Alcoa not to be in violation of the law. Upon appeal, the Supreme Court disqualified itself from the proceedings since it had an insufficient number of justices who could hear the case. Thus, a court of last resort, consisting of a panel of three justices comprised a Court of Appeals which reviewed the case.

In this case, the question of monopoly centered upon a critical definition of the appropriate market. The Alcoa Company produced over 90 percent of virgin aluminum ingot sold in the domestic market and if scrap was included as a part of the market, the company's market share approximated over 60 percent. If scrap was included in the definition of the market, and the company's use of its own ingots were excluded, its calculated market share declined to 33 percent.

The court evaluated these three calculated definitions of Alcoa's appropriate market share.[10]

$$(1)\quad \text{Market Share} = 33\% \quad \frac{\text{Open Market Virgin Ingot + Scrap Ingot}}{\text{Open Market Virgin Ingot + Scarp Ingot + Alcoa's own use Virgin Ingot}}$$

$$(2)\quad \text{Market Share} = 90\% \quad \frac{\text{Open Market Virgin Ingot + Alcoa's own use Virgin Ingot}}{\text{Open Market Virgin Ingot + Alcoa's own use ingot + Imported Ingot}}$$

$$(3)\quad \text{Market Share} = 64\% \quad \frac{\text{Open market Virgin Ingot + Alcoa's own use Virgin Ingot}}{\text{Open Market Virgin Ingot + Alcoa's own use Ingot + Scrap Ingot}}$$

Upon thorough review, Judge Learned Hand concluded that the virgin ingot market was most critical in this case since the aluminum scrap was a derivative of Alcoa's earlier virgin ingot production.

With this definition of the appropriate market, Alcoa's relative share of 90 percent was judged to be excessive and considered a monopoly violation of Sec. 2 of the Sherman Act.

Upon concluding that Alcoa's 90 percent market share was excessive and an illegal monopoly, Judge Hand had to then consider the earlier rule of reason precedent. In this instance, there was no substantial evidence to confirm that Alcoa had achieved its dominant market position through predatory practices or sought to entrench its monopoly position through continued anti-competitive practices. In reversing the rule of reason interpretation he stated:

> "True, it might have been thought adequate to condemn only those monopolies which could not show that they had exercised the highest possible ingenuity, had adopted every possible economy, had anticipated every conceivable improvement, stimulated every possible demand. No doubt, that would be one way of dealing with the matter, although it would imply constant scrutiny and constant supervision, such as courts are unable to provide. Be that as it may, that was not the way that Congress chose; it did not condone "good trust" and condemn "bad" ones, it forbade all.

This precedent setting case established a new judicial test of monopoly that was based solely upon relative-size concentration and the structural characteristics of the firm within the industry. Behavioral considerations and confirming evidence that a firm had abused its dominant market position were no longer of judicial importance in establishing illegality under Section 2. Monopoly size and power itself, however achieved or whatever it may do, is interpretatively illegal under the Sherman Act.

Unlike the court resolutions handed down in the Standard Oil and American Tobacco cases, the court was unwilling to order any punitive remedy against Alcoa. Rather, the court excluded the Company from purchasing any of the available government owned aluminum production facilities which were earlier constructed to meet wartime needs. Thus, its marginal competitors, Kaiser and Reynolds, in acquiring this government surplus property were able to further solidify their competitive position within the industry.

This structural interpretation of Sec. 2 has not been consistently or rigidly applied in more recent years. The courts have been very hesitant to condemn bigness or monopoly as a per se violation unless there is equally some supportive evidence or questionable practices or acts. Their practices need not be blatant examples of abusive or anti-competitive behavior, and might be judged permissible if conducted among smaller- sized companies. Judged within the totality of the situation, the courts have commonly ruled as illegal a dominant firm position which is further supported by questioned forms of behavior which would otherwise be acceptable if pursued by a less conspicuously dominant firm.

U.S. SHOE MACHINERY CO. CASE:

A representative example of this "blended" judicial interpretation is the case involving the United Shoe Machinery Company in 1953. The antitrust division charged that the company had violated Sec. 2 of the Sherman Act by having achieved a market share of 75 to 80 percent of the nation's sales of shoe machinery. From evidence presented, it was clear to the court that the company had achieved its market dominance through research and product development and a proven record of efficient customer service. Equally, the company had not abused its monopoly position through predatory practices and had consistently earned a modest, competitive profit return.

Of pivotal concern to the court were several marketing practices which the company used, which in and of themselves were permissible and not a per se violation of the antitrust laws. For instance, the company only leased its products to customers and obligated the lessee to fully utilize the productive capacity of the leased machine before using a competitor's machine for the same type of manufacturing function. Additionally, the United Shoe Company provided free customer service.

The court ruled that the company was in violation of the law, not because of its excessive market share alone, or because it had introduced any obvious predatory or anti-competitive practices. Indeed, their distribution practices would likely be judged as permissible if conducted by a smaller-sized company. However, this conduct and behavior when combined with the company's size was interpretatively viewed as a violation of the law. The Court stated:

> "They are contracts, arrangements, and policies which, instead of encouraging competition based on pure merit, further the dominance of a particular firm. In this sense, they are unnatural barriers; they unnecessarily exclude actual and potential competition; they restrict a free market...."

> "The violation with which United is now charged depends not on moral considerations, but on solely economic considerations. United is denied the right to exercise control of the market by business policies that are not the inevitable consequences of its capabilities or its natural advantages. That those policies are not immoral is irrelevant.[13]
>
> In all cases, the information obtained was sufficient to inform the defendants of the price they would have to beat in order to obtain a particular sale. Complete market knowledge is certainly not an evil in perfectly competitive markets. This is not, however, such a market, and there is admittedly some danger that nice information will be used for anti-competitive purposes, particularly the maintenance of prices at a high level..." [13]

In sum, the judicial interpretation of the law in this case demands that a firm with substantial market power maintain a record of behavior and conduct that would not necessarily be expected of smaller-sized firms within a more competitive market environment. This seemingly dual evaluative standard dramatizes the inconsistent interpretative nature of the law and the court's hesitancy to use relative-size concentration as the sole determinant of illegality.

RELEVANT GEOGRAPHICAL AND PRODUCT MARKETS:

The question of monopoly power of the attempt to monopolize a market must critically address two evaluative standards: They are (1) The Relevant Geographical Market (The RGM) and (2) The Relevant Product Market (RPM).

While used most frequently to determine the impact and legality of merger activity, these norms are of equal importance in prosecuting an alleged violation of Sec. 2 of the Sherman Act.

The Relevant Geographical Market (RGM) attempts to quantify the territorial bounds within which the firm(s) activities impact. The national market would imply a broad interpretation of the RGM and possibly encompass a larger number of smaller, regional competitors. In contrast, a narrow interpretation might confine the territorial bounds as a distinct section of the country or a regional market. In this instance, a firm may be found in violation of the law because of its impact within a more narrowly defined market area even though it competitively produces and distributes its product throughout the entire country. We will illustrate this important principle when we review several precedent setting merger cases.

The Relevant Product Market (RPM) attempts to identify and measure the unique differentiated, and distinguishable characteristics of the firm's products and relate them to the products of its competitive rivals within the market. A broad interpretation of the RPM would suggest that the firm's product is not significantly unique or differentiated and that there exists a quantifiable degree of product substitutability among consumers within the market. The market demand for the product would then tend to exhibit a relatively high degree of elasticity. A narrower interpretation of the RPM implies that the company's product is distinguishably different from its competitors and that consumers have, for varied reasons differentiated it in their consumption behavior. Under these conditions, market demand for the product would exhibit appreciably more inelasticity.

CROSS ELASTICITY OF DEMAND:

A judicially used measure to quantify the RPM is Cross Elasticity of Demand. This elasticity measure, (Ec), measures the responsiveness of demand for one product when the price of a different product changes. Assuming the products of Firm A and Firm B, the Cross Elasticity concept can be used to determine how the demand for Firm A's product will change when Firm B changes its product price.

$$E_c = \frac{\text{Percentage Change in Quantity Demanded for Product A}}{\text{Percentage Change in Price of Product B}}$$

$$E_c = \frac{dQa}{Q_a} \div \frac{dPb}{P_b} = \frac{dQa}{dP_b} \times \frac{Pb}{Q_a}$$

To illustrate: assume that Firm A's sales increased from 100 to 150 when Firm B increased price from 8 to 10 dollars.

$$E_c = \frac{50}{100} \div \frac{2}{8} = \frac{1}{2} \times \frac{4}{1} = \frac{4}{2} = 2$$

The Cross Elasticity coefficient is +2 which means that Firm A's sales will increase by twice the change in Firm B's selling price. Since Firm B's price rose by 25% (from 8 to 10), then Firm A's sales increased by a multiple of 2, of 50% (from 100 to 150).

In this illustration, the coefficient of Ec is (+) which means that the firms are producing substitutable products and that Firm A's sales will change directly in response to a change in its competitor's (Firm B) price. If Firm B had decreased its price by 25 percent, from 8 to 6 dollars, then Firm A's sales would have declined by 50 percent.

With other data, if a calculation resulted in a negative coefficient, (EC = -), then the products are compliments. There would now exist an inverse relationship between the change in price for one firm's product and the resulting change in demand for the other firm's product. Thus, with a negative coefficient, if Firm A decreased price, that would result in an increase in the demand for product B; or if the price of product A increased, then the demand for Firm B's product would decrease; an inverse relationship.

Thus, a numerically high positive coefficient for Ec would suggest a measured degree of product substitutability within the market and the RPM would be broadly defined. Alternatively, if the coefficient is negative, there is no quantifiable evidence of product substitutability and the RPM would be more narrowly defined.

THE CELLOPHANE CASE:

An important judicial use of this evaluative norm occurred in the so-called Cellophane Case in 1956. The regulatory officials charged the E.I. DuPont de Nemours Co. with having successfully monopolized the nation's production and sale of cellophane in violation of Sec. 2 of the Sherman Act.[14] If the court narrowly defined the RPM to only include cellophane, (inferring that there were no functional wrapping substitutes), the company's market share would approximate 75 percent. In contrast, the company argued that there were many substitutable products, such as aluminum foil and others, and that its sale of cellophane accounted for less than 20 percent of this broader defined market. Following an extensive review and evaluation of prices, qualities, and functional uses, the court concluded that the RPM should be broadly defined, that there were a substantial number of wrapping substitutes, and that the firm's market share of cellophane production was insufficient to constitute an illegal monopoly.

It is important to note that the court in this case, reaffirmed the exclusionary right of patent production. The DuPont Corporation evolved cellophane as a saleable product through its internal research and development efforts. Thus, the company held a patent on cellophane and through contractual arrangement permitted the Sylvania Corp. to produce and sell the remaining 25 percent share of the product market. In its decision, the Court declared that even if the company had possessed excessive and illegal monopoly power, that it would not be subject to prosecution under the Sherman Act since its market dominance was permitted by use of its patent privilege.

Recent litigation against the Xerox Corporation, the American Telephone and Telegraph Company, and the nation's breakfast cereal manufacturers involved the issue of monopolization.

THE XEROX CORPORATION CASE:

In 1973, the Federal Trade Commission charged the Xerox Corporation with having monopolized the nation's copier industry.[15] The Federal Trade Commission's position centered upon Xerox's estimated 86 percent market share of the copier industry and an additional 95 percent share of the plain paper copier industry. It was additionally charged that Xerox's dominant market position evolved from various questionable marketing practices, among them the use of discriminatory quantity discounts among customers, the use of a lease-only policy, and obligating the leasee to contract for the use of Xerox supplies. In addition, the Commission charged that the company had abused its patents as a means of restraining competition to further entrench its monopoly position.

The FTC and the company reached an agreement (consent decree) in July of 1975 which required Xerox to provide its patented technology to its competitors under patent-licensing arrangements. Under the terms of these licensing agreements, Xerox was permitted to secure a royalty fee from the sale of its competitor's products. In addition, Xerox was prohibited from securing any additional patents on copier technology for ten years and had to modify or eliminate some of its questioned marketing practices. Since the agreement was reached, Xerox's market share has declined substantially and the competitive position of its industry rivals has been substantially strengthened.

THE CEREAL INDUSTRY CASE:

The issue of tacit collusion, (The Doctrine of Conscious Parallelism), was the subject of another recent Federal Trade Commission effort to prosecute the nation's cereal industry.[16] This industry is considered highly concentrated and is characterized by a four-firm concentration ratio of over 86 percent. The FTC charged the three largest manufacturers (Kellogg, General Mills, and General Foods) with having an illegal "shared monopoly" position, characterized by unsurmountably high barriers-to-entry. This contention was founded upon the visible lack of price competition, the evident parallel market behavior among the firms, and existence of excessive product differentiation. A main thrust of the Commission's position centered upon the use of advertising as the noted form of industry competition which further heightened entry barriers and contributed to the high level of industry profitability.

In 1981, an FTC Administrative Law Judge recommended that the charges against the companies be dismissed. The Judge argued that the industry's high profitability was consistent with the high level of risk associated with the product. Additionally, the incidence of high advertising expenditures was interpreted as a measure of aggressive market competition among the firms. Lastly, the Judge stated that:

> "Consciously parallel conduct is circumstantial evidence that competitors have acted pursuant to a tacit agreement. Standing alone, however, parallel business behavior does not constitute violation of the antitrust laws..." 16

The historically confirmed distinction between tacit and overt market collusion was once again reaffirmed.

THE AMERICAN TELEPHONE AND TELEGRAPH CASE:

This highly publicized case involved the 1974 Justice Department suit against the American Telephone and Telegraph Company (AT&T).[17] Settled in 1982 by Consent Decree, this case has significant far-reaching implications for the nation's communications industry.

Prior to the decree, AT&T held an estimated 83 percent market share of the nation's telephones. It maintained ownership control over twenty-three local telephone companies and additionally owned the Bell Labs, Western Electric as a vertically integrated equipment manufacturer, and the Bell Long Lines Division.

The Justice Dept. suit charged the company with having evolved an illegal monopoly position by excluding equipment purchases from independent manufacturers that directly competed with Western Electric. In addition, the Justice Dept. alleged that the company sought to purposely restrain the competitive position of its long distance carrier rivals by prohibiting them from interconnecting with the AT&T long distance national based system.

In January 1982, the Justice Dept. and AT&T reached a consent agreement that resulted in the largest divestiture in the nation's regulatory history. Under the terms of the agreement, AT&T was permitted to maintain ownership and control of its three operating subsidiaries: Western Electric, Bell Labs, and The Long Distance Division.

Additionally, it was permitted to competitively enter non-regulated markets. It was required however, to divest ownership over all of the twenty-three local telephone companies that were formerly under its control. In sum, it was estimated that the total market value of the company's divested assets approximated 87 billion dollars.

The decree agreement has significant competitive implications within several different markets. At&T's entry into unregulated markets will intensify competition within the data processing and computer-related industries. Additionally, since the twenty-three companies are no longer under AT&T ownership, it is expected that competition for telephone equipment and long distance telephone business (Sprint, Radium MCT, etc.) will increase substantially.

The cost effect upon the public is uncertain. It is expected that local telephone rates will rise, but may be partially negated since the local companies can charge the entering long distance carriers for interconnection privileges. Overall, the decree has resulted in the entrance of new firms within the communication-related industries and has favorable long-term competitive implications for the nation.

RESTRAINT OF TRADE AND CONSPIRACY:

While Sec. 2 of the Sherman Act is concerned with attempts to monopolize or monopoly power itself, it is Sec. 1 which prohibits various types of "contracts" or "conspiracies" which would contribute to restraint of trade. In interpreting the law, the courts have rather consistently ruled that certain overt practices, such as price-fixing and market-sharing agreements are illegal and they are now considered per se violations. Additionally, with the enactment of the Clayton Act, price discrimination, tying contracts, and exclusive dealerships represent other forms of behavior which are illegal since they restrain trade or "lessen competition...in any line of commerce."

Recall from the earlier discussion of oligopolistic market structures that this industry's behavior, commonly called "mutual interdependence", has been generally ruled permissable under Sec. 1 of the Sherman Act. An uncommunicated awareness among industry firms to pursue identical or parallel market behavior, (the Doctrine of Conscious Parallelism), has been interpreted as an acceptable form of tacit collusion. Thus, it is the process by which uniform prices among competitive rivals evolved that is potentially prosecutable under the law, not the net result itself. An illegality is established when there is recordable evidence of an agreement or purposeful efforts to consummate such agreements.

PRICE-FIXING AGREEMENTS:

One of the more evident examples of such an agreement is direct price-fixing among competitors. Considered a per se violation, this type of conspiracy restrains competition and seriously injures the consuming public.

An early example which illustrated the illegality of this form of market behavior occurred in 1899, when the Supreme Court upheld a decision rendered by the Court of Appeals regarding price-fixing activity among six manufacturers of iron pipe.[18] The companies' conspiracy to avoid price competition by segmenting their markets and maintaining uniformally agreed prices was declared to be a violation of Sec. 1 of the Sherman Act.

SANITARY POTTERS ASSOCIATION CASE:

Another interesting case involved twenty-three corporations which had formed the Sanitary Potters' Association. Manufacturers of pottery fixtures, these firms accounted for 82 percent of the nation's production of fixtures used in bathrooms and lavatories. Initially, a lower district court ruled that the companies had violated Sec. 1 of the Sherman Act because of the introduction of price-fixing agreements. Upon appeal, however, the court of appeals reversed the lower court's decision, arguing that it failed to permit the introduction of evidence which would have supported the companies' contention that their uniform fixed prices were reasonable and not exploitive in nature. Finally, the Supreme Court ruled in support of the earlier district court decision, specifying that the interpretative question of reasonableness was irrelevant. The court stated that the ability of firms to fix prices is itself evidence of illegal market power and should be viewed as a per se violation of the law.[18]

CONTAINER CORPORATION CASE:

In all of the earlier cases in which the courts condemned price-fixing agreements, there was always confirming evidence that the defendants had acted purposely to maintain uncompetitive uniform prices. In the case involving the Container Corporation of America, the Supreme Court extended this consistent interpretation to include the exchange of price information among competitors.[19] In this instance, there was undenied evidence that firms had exchanged price information with each other although there was not any overt arranged understanding to actually fix prices. Rather, the arrangement was limited to an understanding among the competing firms to provide information regarding pricing changes for different products upon request. This exchange of price information was done infrequently and could often be readily secured through permissible market means. Additional evidence presented indicated that these firms accounted for about 90 percent of corrugated container sales within the country and that price differences among them were narrow and limited. Without evidence of an overt price-fixing agreement, the court ruled that this arrangement to exchange pricing information constituted potential restraint of trade and was a violation of Sec. 1 of the Sherman Act. The court stated that:

> "In all cases, the information obtained was sufficient to inform the defendants of the price they would have to beat in order to obtain a particular sale. Complete market knowledge is certainly not an evil in perfectly competitive markets. This is not, however, such a market, and there is admittedly some danger that nice information will be used for anti-competitive purposes, particularly the maintenance of prices at a high level...." 20

Any documentable evidence that confirms an effort among industry firms to eliminate competition among themselves through determined price agreements is the basis for immediate prosecution. The issue of overt price-fixing arrangements as a per se violation of Sec. 1 of the Sherman Act has and continues to be readily re-affirmed by the courts.

There was however, one very interesting exception to this judicial norm.

THE APPALACHIAN COALS CASE:

In response to stagnant and rapidly deteriorating industry conditions, 137 coal producing firms formed Appalachian Coals Inc., in 1929, for the expressed purpose of serving as a single sales agent. This organizational arrangement effectively eliminated competition among these former independent and direct competing firms.

In their defense, the companies argued that this arrangement would preserve the industry's competitive survival since the agreements would foster overall sales through increased advertising and production-distribution cost savings.

Although the evidence clearly confirmed that the real intent was to raise and stabilize prices by controlling output, the Supreme Court upheld the actions of the companies. The court stated:

> "The restrictions the Act imposes are not mechanical or artificial. Its general phases, interpreted to attain its fundamental objects, set up the essential standard of reasonableness. The unfortunate state of the industry would not justify any attempt unduly to restrain competition or to monopolize, but the existing situation prompted defendants to make, and the statute did not preclude them from making, an honest effort to remove abuses, to make competition fairer, and thus to promote the essential interests of commerce. The interests of producers and consumers are linked." 21

This judicial interpretation has not been reaffirmed in subsequent cases involving overt price-fixing arrangements. It does suggest, however, that a norm of interpretative reasonableness may be used in defense of this form of market behavior if it ultimately ensures the: (1) competitive survival of the firms and industry and (2) the long-term interests of the user population.

TRADE ASSOCIATION ACTIVITIES AND THE ANTITRUST LAWS:

There exists a large number of trade associations whose membership consists of competing firms within different industries. Trade associations are permissible, and the regulatory dilemma becomes one of determining those forms of association activities which enhance the member companies competitive position from those which illegally erode competition within the industry. Trade associations serve many important and useful functions, among them, a depository of industry and market information such as: the credit worthiness of customers, industry sales and production statistics, quality standards, research and new product development, projected changes in industry or market conditions, and promotion of the interest of the industry and its members to its labor and governmental constituency. In providing these services and sources of information, trade associations can advance the economic interests of the industry and further the competitive potential of its individual member firms. These forms of activities have and continue to be immune from antitrust prosecution.

However, the courts have consistently condemned those forms of association activities that have enabled its member companies to restrain competition through the imposition of uniform prices or the establishment of production and sales quotas.

THE SUGAR INSTITUTE CASE:

The Sugar Institute, Inc. was a trade association comprising manufacturers of refined sugar which together accounted for over 80 percent of total market sales. The regulatory officials charged that the member firms violated Sec. 1 of the Sherman Act since the association obligated its members to publicize their selling prices in advance of sales and to keep their prices unalterably firm until further pricing changes occurred. The evidence presented confirmed that the association was formed to discourage competing firms from granting price concessions to large buyers and ultimately stabilize pricing policies within the industry. Without recordable evidence of a conspiracy to fix prices, the Supreme Court ruled that the interpretative intent of the association sponsored arrangement requiring its members to maintain rigidly fixed prices and their announced pricing plans was illegal.[22]

TAG MANUFACTURERS CASE:

In Tag Manufacturers Institute v. Federal Trade Commission, the association, acting on behalf of its membership, requested that the Appeals Court reverse a Commission ruling that its activities violated Sec. 5 of the FTC Act concerning an "unfair method of competition." The member companies, manufacturers of tag products, accounted for approximately 95 percent of total industry production and sales with the four largest firms having a market share of almost 55 percent. The questioned practice involved an understanding among the member firms to daily report to the association the selling prices, terms of sale, and any changes in pricing decisions for all of its products. It was estimated that over 80 percent of the members' sales was made to order or custom type business. Upon receipt of this sales information, the association mailed bulletins to all of its members indicating all off-list transactions. The published bulletin identified the seller, the type of customed tag product, the quantity sold, the list price and the actual purchase price.

Evidence presented confirmed that the submission of price lists and other sales information had been consistently adhered to since the Institute's founding in 1933. Indeed, industry members evolved so-called Tag Industry Agreements in 1935, 1936, 1937, and 1940. These agreements were primarily concerned with the compilation and dissemination of industry-related statistics and obligated the member firms to report prices and terms of sale for all tag product transactions. The court concluded that the association's reporting requirements were historically established and "once a price list has been issued to the trade it necessarily becomes pretty much public information." The Tag Industry Agreement merely facilitates the assembling of such data. As to the obligation of subscribers to report off-list sales and to furnish copies of invoices, that is no more than the reporting of past transactions. The Commission had endeavored to show that the agreement was something more than this, that it was a price-fixing agreement having the purpose and actual effect of restraining and preventing price competition. We believe that such findings are unsupported by the evidence or by any reasonable inferences to be drawn therefrom." 23 In sum, the court ruled that these contested practices were not a violation of the law and set aside the cease and desist order imposed by the FTC.

TYING CONTRACT:

Under the provisions of the Clayton Act, price discrimination, reciprocity and tying contracts are illegal since they constitute a practice which can "lessen competition."

Recall, a tying contract obligates a buyer or leasee to purchase or lease additional and unwanted products or services as a condition to finalize the transaction. The courts have consistently condemned this type of business practice as excessive market abuse and have decreed it as an example of illegal monopoly dominance.

NORTHERN PACIFIC RAILROAD COMPANY CASE:

The illegality of a tying contract arrangement was the focal issue in the Northern Pacific Railroad Company v. U.S. case.[24]

The Congress in 1864 and 1870 granted the company over forty million acres of land in the northwestern region of the country to expedite the construction of railroad facilities. Over the year, the company sold some of the land and leased other parcels to be used notably for agricultural-related purposes. The judicial issue in this case involved an interpretation of the "preferential routing" clause which the company inserted in all of its sales and lease contracts. Specifically, the clause obligated the new owner or leasee to transport all of its products derived from the land on the company's railroads, provided that its charges were comparable to the rates of its competitors. The Supreme Court ruled that this contractual obligation could contribute to restraint of trade and was in violation of the law.

SINCLAIR REFINING COMPANY CASE:

In another case involving tying contract arrangements, the FTC filed a complaint against the Sinclair Refining Company, charging a violation of Sec. 3 of the Clayton Act.[25] The questioned practice involved the companys' lease agreement to furnish underground gas storage tanks to independent gas station owners at minimal rental rates if the stations agreed to exclusively sell gasoline supplied by Sinclair.

In this instance, the Supreme Court permitted the tying arrangement since the low rental charge for the use of the storage tanks minimized the capitalization requirements needed to enter the industry. The court suggested that the arrangement's permissibleness in this instance, was centered on its having possibly diminished the financial barriers to entry and ultimately culminated in intensifying competition within the industry. It is important to note that the judicial decision rendered in this case is a limited exception to the court's consistent interpretation of the per se illegality of tying arrangements.

EXCLUSIVE DEALERSHIPS:

Recall that exclusive dealerships as well as tying contracts are illegal under Sec. 3 of the Clayton Act if they lessen competition and contribute to monopoly market conditions. Exclusive dealing involves a contractual or oral agreement between a seller and buyer to make the seller's product available for sale if the buyer agrees not to equally sell a competitor's products. Unlike the readiness of the courts to vigorously prosecute tying contracts, exclusive dealerships have been permitted under those conditions where they were proven to have intensified market competition.

STANDARD OIL COMPANY OF CALIFORNIA CASE:

An early case involving the illegality of exclusive dealerships involved the Standard Oil Company of California in 1949.[26] In this instance, the Supreme Court reviewed, upon appeal, the decision of a lower District Court that the company had violated Sec. 3 of the Clayton Act through the illegal use of exclusive dealer arrangements.

Standard Oil of California owned refining plants in California and distributed gasoline and other petroleum-based products to its own service stations, to the owners of independent stations, and to industrial users throughout the Western states. The company accounted for 23 percent of all wholesaled gasoline within its area. Of its total market share, 6.8% of all company sales were to its own service stations, an additional 6.7 percent were through exclusive-dealership contracts with independently owned stations, and the remainder were to industrial users. The company's six largest competitors had a total market share of 42.5 percent and the remaining 34.5 percent market share was absorbed by an additional seventy small companies. At issue were the exclusive-dealing arrangements which the company had consummated with about 8,000 independently owned stations which obligated the owners to exclusively sell Standard Oil of California petroleum products and in some instances, tires, batteries and other products.

The Supreme Court affirmed the lower court's decision and ruled that the company's exclusive-dealership arrangements lessened the competitive position of its rivals and were a violation of the law.

Whether exclusive dealerships are judged permissible or illegal is critically dependent upon the judicial interpretation of the relevant geographical market. In the Standard Oil of California case, the court narrowly limited the market bounds to the Western states and considered the dominance of the company within a more limited definition of the market; involving independently owned stations.

THE TAMPA ELECTRIC COMPANY CASE:

The interpretative definition of the relevant market was of equal importance in determining the legality of an exclusive-dealership contract in 1961. Upon appeal, the Supreme Court reviewed a breach of contract case between the Nashville Coal Co. and the Tampa Electric Co.[27]

The Tampa Electric Co., an electric utility located in Tampa, Florida, had two oil based generating facilities. In 1955, the company constructed an additional generating plant that was coal-fired and contracted with the Nashville Coal Co. to supply coal for a twenty year period. The agreed contract between the two firms made the Nashville Coal Co. the exclusive supplier of coal during the term of the agreement. Because of increases in coal prices, Nashville realized that the contracted arrangement with Tampa Electric would not be sufficiently profitable and refused to honor its delivery obligations on the grounds that the agreement was a violation of antitrust law. The Tampa Electric Co. brought private litigation against the company to force it into meeting its contract supply obligations. The Nashville Coal Co. argued that its supply obligations to Tampa Electric would be equal to the total consumption of coal (700,000 tons) used throughout the entire state. Since its contract made it the exclusive supplier, the company argued that this violated antitrust law since it would negate or exclude its competitors from a large portion of total market sales. In contrast, the Tampa Electric Co. argued that the relevant market area should include a broader eight state area and that this contracted agreement would now comprise less than 1 percent of total market sales.

The Supreme Court affirmed the lower court's broad interpretation of the market and ruled that this exclusive arrangement was not a violation of law.

In general, the legality of exclusive-dealer arrangements are also subject to the "reasonableness" interpretation of the court. They are not viewed as predictable per se violations, but rather, the length and flexibleness of the agreement, the relative size of the firms involved, and the territorial bounds of the defined market area all affect the final judicial decision. A contractual agreement that involves at least one dominant firm within a definably concentrated industry is likely to be judged in violation of the law, particularly if the arrangement is determined to impact upon a measurable portion of the market. In contrast, agreements which impact upon a negligible share of the market and involve smaller-sized firms within a relatively competitive industry are less likely to be illegal. Such was the case involving the contractual dispute between Nashville and Tampa Electric in which Nashville was determined to be 1 of 700 potential suppliers.

SUMMARY:

The nation's initial antitrust initiative was a response to the early stage of industrialization and with it the emergence of monopolistic elements within the economy. The Sherman Act, legislated in 1890, addressed the issues of restraint of trade and monopoly within interstate commerce. Subsequent legislation: The Clayton Act, FTC Act, and The Celler-Kefauver Act addressed several specific forms of abusive market behavior and the issue of merger activity.

The forceful application of the law's provisions are critically dependent upon judicial interpretation. The Rule of Reason Doctrine emphasized behavioral and performance norms as a test of monopoly and negated any consideration of the structural characteristics of the industry. The Reversed Rule of Reason Doctrine, first introduced in the Alcoa Case, negated behavioral characteristics and judged monopoly solely on the basis of structural conditions within the industry. Monopoly, whether good or bad, is illegal.

FOOTNOTES

1. U.S. v. E.C. Knight Co., 156 U.S. 1 (1895).

2. Federal Trade Commission v. Raladam Co., 283 U.S. 643 (1931). In this case, the Supreme Court ruled that the Raladam Co. had not violated earlier antitrust laws since it was not proven that the possible harmful and falsely advertised remedy had equally injured the competitive position of other firms.

Footnotes Continued

3. Standard Oil Company of New Jersey v. U.S., 221 U.S.1 (1911).

4. Ibid, p. 63-66.

5. U.S. v. American Tobacco Co., 221 U.S. 106 (1911).

6. U.S. v. U.S. Steel Corp., 251 U.S. 417 (1920).

7. Ibid., pp. 450-451.

8. U.S. v. American Can Co., 230 F. 859,861 (1916).

9. United States v. Aluminum Company of America, 148 F. 2nd 416 (2nd Cir., 1945).

10. Eugene M. Singer, Antitrust Economics and Legal Analysis, Grid Publishing Co., Columbus, Ohio, p.55.

11. U.S. v. Aluminum Company of America, in Singer, p.57.

12. United States v. United Shoe Machinery Co. of New Jersey, 347, U.S. 521 (1954).

13. Ibid, pp. 344-345.

14. U.S. v. E.I. DuPont de Nemours & Co., 351 U.S. 377 (1956).

15. Federal Trade Commission v. Xerox Corporation, 86 F.T.C. 364 (1975).

16. Federal Trade Commission v. Kellogg, FTC Docket 8883 (1981).

17. United States v. American Telephone and Telegraph Company Consent Decree (1982).

18. Addyston Pipe and Steel Company v. U.S., 175 U.S. 211 (1899).

19. U.S. v. Container Corporation of America, et al., 393 U.S. 333 (1969).

20. Ibid, p.20.

21. Appalachian Coals, Inc. v. United States, 228 U.S. 344 (1933).

Footnotes Continued

22. The Sugar Institute, Inc. v. U.S., 297 U.S. 553 (1936).

23. Tag Manufacturers Institute v. Federal Trade Commission, 174 F. 2d 452 (1st Cir. 1949).

24. Northern Pacific Railroad Company v. United States, 356 U.S. 1 (1958).

25. Federal Trade Commission v. Sinclair Refining Co., 261 U.S. 463 (1923).

26. Standard Oil Company of California (and Standard Stations Inc.,) v. United States, 337 U.S. 293 (1949).

27. Tampa Electric Co. v. Nashville Coal Co., 365 U.S. 320 (1961).

CHAPTER READINGS

Blair, John, M. Economic Concentration: Structure, Behavior and Public Policy, Harcourt Brace Jovanovich, Inc. New York, 1972, Chap. 5,6.

Greer, Douglas, F. Industrial Organization and Public Policy, MacMillan Publishing Co., New York, 1980. Chap. 4,5.

Koch, James. V. Industrial Organization and Prices, Prentice-Hall, Inc., Englewood Cliffs, N.J. 1974. Chap. 9,10.

Gergacz, Joh, and Whitman, Douglas, The Legal and Social Environment of Business, Random House, New York, 1985, Chap. 13,14,15,16.

Petersen, H. Craig, Business and Government, Harper and Row, Publisher, New York, 1981. Chap. 5,6,7.

Shepard, William and Wilcox, Clair, Public Policies Toward Business Richard D. Irwin Inc., 6th Ed. 1979, Chap. 6.

CHAPTER FOUR

STATUTES AND POLICIES WHICH IMPEDE COMPETITION

The enactment and enforcement of the antitrust laws is supported by the implied legal mandate embodied in the Interstate Commerce Clause of the nation's constitution. As earlier noted, regulatory policy seeks to approximate and preserve a competitive market environment so that the market system remains responsive to the interests and needs of the nation's populace. Thus, it strives to ensure the efficient, least-cost allocation of resources into production and the least-price distribution of finished goods into consumption.

However, in response to a perceived national economic need or an evolved market situation, the Congress has enacted several statutes which are contrary to the regulatory intent of the antitrust laws. This legislation has provided a shelter from antitrust prosecution for many firms in diverse industries. In so doing, it has and continues to permit various types of practices and forms of industry conduct which would be otherwise prosecuted as per se violations of the law. Rather than promoting a competitive market environment, these legislative exemptions erodeb business rivalry and promote monopolistic behavior. These legislative departures impact upon the manufacturing, agricultural, and retail sectors and additionally affect oceanic transportation. Regarding the latter, the Shipping Act of 1916 grants authority to the Federal Maritime Commission to provide antitrust immunity for agreements consummated among ocean ship owners. Additionally, the Copper-Vol-Stead Act, legislated in 1922, permits the formation of producer cooperatives among farmers as a means of stabilizing the controlled distribution of agricultural products. This exemption was intended to provide farmers with more direct and discretionary control over supply conditions so as to insulate them against erratic fluctuations in the market.

WEBB-POMERENE EXPORT TRADE ACT:

The Webb-Pomerene Act was legislated in 1918 with the anticipation that it would strengthen the competitive position of smaller sized domestic businesses in their efforts to penetrate foreign markets. Under the Act's provisions, rival firms within an industry are permitted to form an export trade association that is then registered with the FTC. As a means of enhancing their export potential, various types of overt marketing and distribution practices are condoned that would otherwise be decreed as per se violations if directed towards the domestic market. Participating firms may permissibly fix export prices and further strive to eliminate export-oriented competition among themselves through the establishment of market-sharing and sale quota agreements. In sum, this exemptive legislation sponsors domestically formed export-oriented cartels.

As expressed in the Act, these collusive practices are allowable as long as they do not artificially depress domestic market conditions. Additionally, in response to an inquiry from an association, the FTC declared in 1945, that the Webb-Pomerene organizations could permissibly enter into restrictive agreements with foreign cartels. This evident misinterpretation of the legislation's intent was readily rescinded.

The historical record suggests that the Webb-Pomerene Act has not significantly benefitted the export sales performances of the nation's smaller-sized businesses. Rather, the noted benefactors of this exemptive shelter have been relatively large, dominant-sized firms within very concentrated industries. Table I illustrates the level of industry concentration on the basis of the Kaysen and Turner classification among those domestic industries that have formed export trade associations. Among the thirty-three different industries which have been represented, 21 have been of the highly concentrated Type I oligopolistic form and an additional 6 associations have been of the equally concentrated Type II form.

A Type I oligopoly market is one in which the eight largest producers account for at least 50 percent but less than 75 percent of total industry sales. The twenty largest firms account for at least 75 percent of total industry sales. A Type II oligopoly is one in which the eight largest producers account for at least thirty-three but less than 50 percent of total industry sales and the twenty largest account for at least 50 but less than 75 percent of total industry sales.

Table 1

Concentration Among Webb-Pomerene Association Member Industries

Industry Group	Type I Oligopoly	Type II Oligopoly	Unconcentrated
Agricultural	3	3	1
Metal Products	6	-	1
Mine Products	6	-	1
Lumber Products	1	-	2
Other Manufacturers (Rubber Tires, Steel, Locomotives)	5	2	1
	21	6	6

On average, total annual exports from Webb-Pomerene assisted firms have approximated less than 4 percent of the nation's total export volume and have been largely attributable to the activity of recognizable large-sized firms for whom the legislation was not intended. A subcommittee of the U.S. Senate reported in 1946:

> "The expected advantages for small business from participation in export associations have rarely materialized, that only rarely and under special circumstances can small business benefit from the Webb-Pomerene Act, and that the preponderent effect of the Act seems to have been to facilitate the concentration of industrial power in the hands of large enterprises to the detriment of small existing or potential competitors." [1]

It is evident that this attempt to construct a standard which seeks to distinguish between allowable competitive restraints in export trade and similar illegal restraints in domestic commerce among the same rival firms has not fulfilled its legislative intent.

An interesting case involving Webb-Pomerene Trade Association was settled by the Supreme Court in 1968. The U.S. Phosphate Trade Association was comprised of domestic fertilizer manufacturers who submitted a fixed price offer to supply the government of South Korea with a large shipment of fertilizer to be financed under the U.S. foreign aid program. While the submission of a non-competitive fixed-price bid among the member firms was permissible under the Act, the interpretative question centered on the definition of what constitutes an export trade transaction. The Supreme Court decreed that this sale did not constitute foreign trade since it was to be financed by the United States Government and therefore it did not come under the exemptive provisions of the Webb-Pomerene Act. The firms were thus obligated to submit individually derived, competitive price bids.

COMMERCIAL TRADE POLICY INSTRUMENTS:

While not within the strict definitional umbrella of legislative exemptions, it is evident that various commercial trade policy measures that the national government imposes equally serve to diminish the intensity of competition within domestic markets. The imposition of import quotas which directly restrict foreign supply and the widespread use of various types of tariffs which inflate the selling prices of imported goods all erode the intensity of competition within domestic industries.

Import quotas have become increasingly popular because of their predictable effect. They establish an upper bound in either physical or nominal values as to the amount of the foreign produced product that can be imported into a nation. The relatively recent quotas that the U.S. voluntarily negotiated with the Japanese government limits the amounts of textile-related products and automobiles that Japanese manufacturers may export to the U.S. market.

TARIFFS:

A tariff is a tax imposed upon foreign produced products that are being imported into a nation. Whether of an Ad Valorem, Specific, or Compound nature, all imposed tariffs inflate the selling price of the imported product. An Ad Valorem Levy is expressed as a percent of market value; a Specific Levy is a fixed financial sum on each physical unit of the product imported, and a Compound Tariff is a combination of both types of levies. The anticipated effect is to increase the imported good's selling price to discourage domestic consumption and thereby protect domestic industry. Fig. I illustrates the various effects of an imposed tariff.

Fig. I

IMPACT OF TARIFF

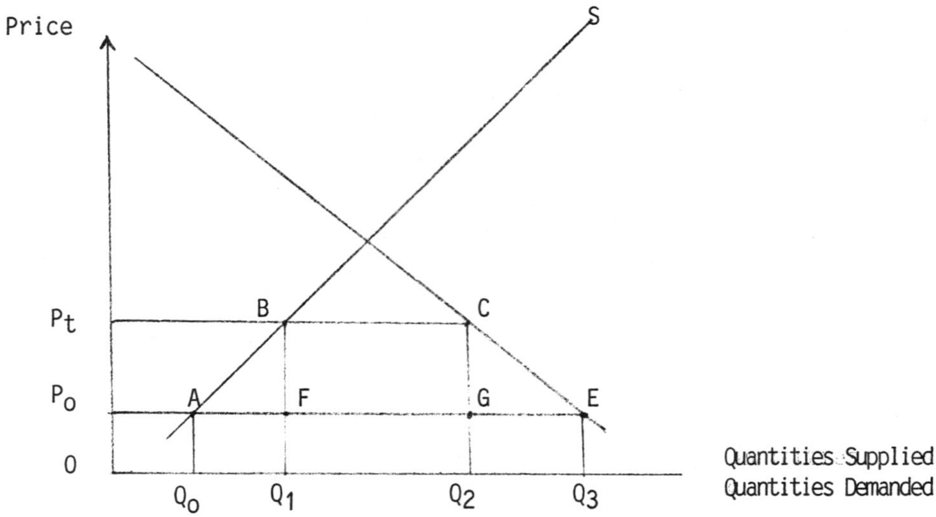

The diagram illustrates domestic demand and domestic supply conditions. Before the imposition of the tariff, the imported product's selling price in the domestic market is OPo. At this initial pre-tariff price, total domestic consumption is OQ_3 and that portion of total demand satisfied by domestic producers equals OQo. The difference between domestic demand and that portion met by domestic manufacturers is $Qo-Q_3$ which represents the total level of imports prior to the tariff. An imposed tariff, like any tax, increases the selling price of the imported product from OPo to OPt which contracts domestic demand from OQ_3 to OQ_2. The decrease in domestic consumption ($Q_2 - Q_3$), commonly called the Consumption Effect will substantially restrict imports if the import demand function is elastic in nature. The higher post-tariff price (OPt) will equally stimulate domestic production which increases from OQo to OQ_1. This rise in domestic manufacturing is called the Production or Protective Effect since it depicts the added domestic supply response when insulated from foreign competition. After the tariff has been imposed, total imports approximate a more limited Q_1-Q_2 in response to the restrictive consumption and expanded production effects.

The revenue which accrues to the government is dependent upon the unit value of the tariff, (Po-Pt), and the quantity of import products (Q_1-Q_2) upon which it is imposed. Thus, total revenue receipts, or the Revenue Effect approximates the area, BCFG.

Another very important impact of levied tariffs is the net transfer or redistribution of wealth from one segment of the economy to another. Prior to the tariff, domestic manufacturers produced at the pre-tariff price OPo. Thus, total revenue which accrued to domestic firms approximated the area OPo AQo. After the tariff has been imposed, total domestic supply equals OQl and is sold at the higher post-tariff price of OPt. Domestic manufacturers now realize a higher revenue flow which equals the area OPt + BQ_1. Higher total production costs are incurred by domestic manufacturers because of the increase in domestic supply (Qo-Ql). The total increase in domestic manufacturing costs is measured by this net gain in production (Q_o-Q_1) times the marginal costs of producing the additional output which is represented by the respective points A and B on the domestic supply function. Thus, the total increased manufacturing costs incurred is equal to the quantity of increased output (Qo-Ql) times marginal cost (A-B) or Q_oABQ_1. The amount by which the gain in total revenue exceeds the increase in total costs of production, (P_oP_tBA), is referred to as the <u>Redistribution Effect</u>, and represents the net transfer of wealth from the consumer to producer segments of the economy.

The arguments in support of or against tariffs and other forms of commercial policy instruments are immediately relevant and have and continue to be exhaustively debated. They are noted within the context of our discussion because they can and do measurably impact upon the incidence and intensity of competition within domestic markets.

<u>EXPORT TRADING COMPANIES</u>:

An additional antitrust exemption for domestic companies engaged in export trade was provided with the passage of the Export Trading Company Act in October, 1982. Also intended to promote the export potential of the nation's smaller businesses, the legislation permits firms within the same industries to form an Export Trading Company as an organization for joint export sales. The legislation permits bank holding companies to assume a direct ownership and participatory vote and obligates an ETC to perform only one role, as either a vehicle for direct exportation of goods and services or for providing export-related services. Unlike the Webb-Pomerene Act, the Act permits cooperative export arrangements in the foreign sale of services in addition to merchandise wares.

The initiative for this legislation was precipitated by two concerns: (1) an awareness that smaller-sized businesses had not fulfilled their export potential because of cost, risk and managerial considerations, and (2) that domestic businesses were hesitant to form joint agreements because of the fear of possible antitrust prosecution. In addressing this concer, the Act requires the Justice Department to evaluate a proposed ETC and certify its immunity from prosecution. Once certification has been granted the member firms are assured that their activities will not be subject to antitrust litigation, except possible legal action initiated by a private party. Upon review, the Justice Department will grant certification and prosecutable immunity when it confirms that:[2]

(1) the ETC's activities will not result in a substantial lessening of competition or restraint of trade within the domestic market or of any competitive rivals;

(2) the ETC's activities do not unreasonably affect the domestic price of those exported goods and services;

(3) the ETC's activities do not constitute or contribute to unfair methods of competition which adversely impact upon competitors within the domestic market, and

(4) the ETC's activities must exclusively apply to the exportation of goods and services and cannot culminate in the direct sale or resale of the exports within the domestic economy.

In the course of determining certification eligibility, the question of what constitutes an unacceptable, in contract to permissible "lessening of competition" or "unreasonable affect on domestic prices" is interpretatively difficult. The process itself implies an erosion of regulatory standards. However, if the legislation successfully promotes the export performance of smaller-sized firms it may ultimately invigorate their overall competitive position within the domestic industry. Through this means, the intensity of competition among all firms within domestic industries may be enhanced.

EXEMPTIONS IN RETAIL TRADE:

While accelerated technological advances and new innovations transformed the nation's manufacturing sector during the early decades of the 20th century, there were also revolutionary changes in retail marketing and distribution. Historically characterized by a general store, the retail sector rapidly evolved from the countless number of small, family operated establishments to the dominance of a small number of large volume, discount-priced, merchandising chains. The growth of the so-called "chain stores" was spectacular and they accounted for an estimated 30 percent of all retail trade activity by 1969.[3] This success threatened the very economic survival of the small, independently owned retail establishments throughout the country. In their defense, the mass distributors argued that they were able to accrue significant cost economies and, to the betterment of the consumer, were able to competitively retail their products at prices substantially below the prices charged by the small retail establishments. While there was widespread evidence that the chains often abused their volume buying leverage, it became readily evident that the small, marginal retailers were not able to effectively compete.

Largely in response to a nationally organized lobbyist effort, the Congress enacted several exemptive statutes that attempted to advance the competitive survival of small retailers. This legislation included the Robinson-Patman Act of 1936, the Miller-Tydings of 1937 and the McQuire-Keough Act of 1952.

The Miller-Tydings Act of 1937 provided an exemption to manufacturers and retailers from prosecution under Sec. 1 of the Sherman Act and represented the legal means by which individual states could enact and enforce the Fair-Trade or Price Maintenance Laws. When enacted at the discretion of individual states, the Fair-Trade laws prescribed the minimum retail price at which a manufacturer's product could be sold regardless of whether it was purchased at a discount chain or a small retail store. This denied the large merchandisers the opportunity to pass their lower costs on to the consumers by discounting the product's price. In general it resulted in uniform prices within all retail outlets for those products which were fair traded and prevented consumers from making selective price choices.

This retail practice was strengthened in 1952 with the passage of the McQuire-Keough Act which contained the "non-signer" clause. In sum, it obligated all retail establishments to adhere to a contractually agreed selling price on a fair-traded product when the contract was consummated between the manufacturer and one retailer within the state. This statute strengthened the exemptive intent embodied in the Miller-Tydings Act which sought to ensure the uneconomic survival of inefficient retailers throughout the country. While estimates of excessive price costs vary, it is reasonable to conclude that the history of fair-trade resulted in billions of inflated charges to the nation's consumers.

Finally, the Congress enacted the Consumer Goods Pricing Act in 1976 which repealed the earlier enacted Miller-Tydings Law. Without this exemptive umbrella, the states could no longer legally enact and enforce their fair-trade laws. Thus, this very controversial chapter in the nation's regulatory history came to an end.

THE ROBINSON-PATMAN ACT:

The Robinson-Patman Act, legislated in 1936, represented an additional legislative attempt to competitively protect and ensure the survival of the nation's smaller retailers. Enforced by the

Federal Trade Commission, the Act amended the Sec. 2 price-discrimination provision of the Clayton Act to lessen the permissible quantity discounts that could be granted to high volume merchandise buyers.

Recall that Sec. 2 of the Clayton Act prohibits price discrimination unless justified by recordable differences in quantities purchased. Permissible quantity discounts resulted in substantial cost savings to the volume-purchasing chains and eroded the competitive position of the small independent retailers. Thus, the Act sought to restrict allowable price discrimination against or in favor of the large-volume chain stores. Its noted provision prohibits a seller from discriminating in price among different buyers of products of similar quality and grade when the result "may be substantially to lessen competition or tend to create a monopoly in any line of commerce." Additionally, the law decrees that price differences among buyers of different quantities is illegal if this condition provingly results in "injury or destroys or prevents competition with any person who either grants or knowingly receives the benefits of such discrimination." Thus, price discrimination is illegal when it injures or destroys competition among rival firms, as well as when it contributes to lessened competition in the market. The FTC has the authority to establish maximum quantity discounts to ensure the protective intent of this provision.

In an effort to prohibit any monopsony abuses which the volume buyers might seek in their purchase agreements, the Robinson-Patman Act forbids special discounts, or promotional advertising allowances to one buyer unless these sale concessions are equally available to all buyers on an equitable and proportional basis.

The Robinson-Patman Act is very controversial and has often been recommended for repeal. Unsubstantiated differences in price which abusively erode a competitor's position within the market or which lessen competition within an industry should be rightfully condemned. However, not permitting price discrimination which is attributable to accountable differences in quantities sold, transportation, or production costs is unjustified reverse price discrimination. This latter condition is equally injurious to businesses and notably penalizes the consuming public which should likely benefit from lower product prices.

There are evident benefits which have derived from the legislation. It has obligated manufacturers to carefully scrutinize their marketing practices to ensure that their purchase discount and promotional concessions offered to buyers correspond to realized costs and are thus equitable. In this regard, it has somewhat restored the competitive vitality of the nation's smaller retailers and ensured that the volume discount chains have not exercised abusive buying behavior or extracted illegal concessions because of their dominant market position. Overall, however, the law has substantially reduced the benefits of volume buying, injected confusion and interpretative uncertainty in buyer-seller relationships, and has diminished the intensity of retail price competition. Philosophically it constitutes a very questionable digression from the legislative intent of the nation's antitrust laws. Regulatory policy seeks to properly preserve a competitive market environment and to insulate consumers against the predatory market abuses of businesses. The Robinson-Patman Act, like that of other exemptive retail legislation seeks foremost to protect one segment of the business community from another, without normative regard to the impact of this skewed policy upon the consuming public.

JUDICIAL INTERPRETATION OF THE LAW:

There has been a substantial amount of litigation brought by the FTC under the Robinson-Patman Act. During the course of judicial review, one or more of the following legal defenses have been used to test the interpretative applicability of the law.

(1) The firm may argue that the differences in price among buyers represents differences in "grade or quality", or simply, that they are not the same products being sold. This is allowable under the law.

(2) The firm might argue that it selectively lowered its price to match the existing competitive price of a rival from within its market. The company may argue that this pricing response reflects its "good faith" intentions to preserve its competitive market position and was not intended to "substantially lessen competition."

(3) The questioned lowering of price might constitute a deliberate decision to lower the price of inventory stocks which might be perishable or unsaleable at a later date because of obsolescene. Businesses may permissibly liquidate their stocks of unsold goods by offering them for sale at unprofitable price levels. This form of allowed discriminatory pricing must be sporadic, short-lived, and not a continuous characteristic of the company's distribution policy.

(4) The company might argue that the price differences among its customers reflects the recordable differences in transportation and distribution costs. Geographical differences can justify price variances when the price differences are a measure of differences in distribution and servicing costs.

FTC v. ANHEUSER-BUSCH CASE:

In the Federal Trade Commission v. Anheuser-Busch, Inc. case, the Supreme Court reviewed the issue of primary-line discrimination and confirmed the applicableness of the Robinson-Patman Act to firms injured by the discriminatory pricing practices of an industry competitor.[4] The company typically sold its premier product, Budweiser, at a higher price than competitive products within different regional markets. For purposes of promoting its premium product, the company lowered its price to match the lower prices of its regional competitors in the St. Louis, Missouri market. To achieve its promotional objective, the company did not discriminate among its buyers within the St. Louis market, but rather offered the same discounted price to all potential buyers. In contrast, the company continued to charge higher prices to all customers not located within the limitedly defined St. Louis market. The company's promotional strategy successfully increased sales by over 200 percent from the levels of the preceding year.[5] The Supreme Court ruled that the company had violated the Robinson-Patman Act for having its product at different prices within the different market areas.

CORN PRODUCTS REFINING COMPANY CASE:

The Corn Products Refining Company v. Federal Trade Commission proceedings addressed the legality of a company using a pricing mechanism based upon a based delivery point.[6] The Corn Product Co. manufactured glucose in a Chicago facility that was sold to candy manufacturers. After it constructed an additional glucose manufacturing facility in Kansas City, the company continued to sell its product (regardless of which plant manufactured it) at a price which used Chicago as its basing point. Thus, the product made in Kansas City and sold to Kansas City customers would sell at a price which included transportation costs from the Chiccago plant to the point of sale. Alternatively, Chicago based customers were charged lower prices since the sale incorporated transportation charges derived from the Chicago-based delivery point. The court ruled that the candy manufacturers in both geographic locations are in direct competition with each other and that this discriminatory pricing policy lessened industry competition in violation of the law.

THE SUN OIL CASE:

In the Sun Oil v. FTC case, the Supreme Court considered the issue of a firm offering a discriminatory lower price to meet existing competition.[7] The Sun Oil Company lowered its wholesale price to one independent dealer (McLean), an operator of Sunoco gas stations in Jacksonville, Florida, to match the low price offered by a near-by discount gas station. The Sun Oil Company did not make similar wholesale price concessions available to other customers within the market area. More notably, the Supreme Court ruled that the company had violated the Robinson-Patman Act since it was primarily engaged in wholesale and not retail business. The Court noted that its lower price to McLean would have been permissible if it had responded to a lower price offer to another competitive wholesaler who was seeking to secure McLean's business from Sun Oil. Reducing a product price to match a competitor's lower price as a means of maintaining a firm's market position is allowable under the law. However, in this instance, the Court noted that Sun Co. illegally lowered price as a wholesaler and was not directly in competition with the independent discount gas station at the retail level. If determined not to be directly engaged in retail trade, the company could not legally lower its price to meet a different level of competition under the provision of the Robinson-Patman ACt. The Court stated:

> "We see no reason to permit Sun discriminatorily to pit its greater strength at the supplier level against Super Test, which so far as appears from the record, is able to sell its gasoline at a lower price simply because it is a more efficient merchandiser, particularly when Super Test's challenge as an "independent" may be the only meaningful source of price competition offered by the "major" oil companies, of which Sun is one.[8]

<u>THE MORTON SALT CO. CASE</u>:

The law's intent to preserve the competitive survival of small retailers is represented in a case involving the Morton Salt Co.[9] The Morton Salt Co., a manufacturer of refined salt, charged its volume buyers substantially lower prices than those offered to its lesser customers. While the company sought to justify its pricing policy as attributable to quantity and transportational cost differences, the Supreme Court determined that its marketing policy had contributed substantial injury to the small businesses. The cost disparity was so great that the larger buyers were often able to profitably sell the finished product at a price which was less than that charged by Morton Salt to the marginal businesses. As evidenced by this case, price discrimination, when justified for cost reasons, may still be illegal if it seriously injures or potentially results in the elimination of competition.

PATENTS:

Our nation's forefathers wisely recognized the importance of promoting technological and innovative advances. Indeed, as the nation's history has unfolded, it is evident that the advances in technology and the continuous introduction of innovations have been the major contributors to industrial growth and an unsurpassed standard-of-living. It was with this sense of vision that the nation's first patent law was enacted in 1790. This was followed by the establishment of the Patent Office in 1836.

A Patent has a limiting restraint on competition since it imposes a 17 year monopoly privilege to its holder over the manufacture and distribution of a product or process. The patent provides legal protection to ensure that no other individual or business can reproduce for sale the product or process unless sanctioned by the original holder. In sum, the patent provides for an exclusive monopoly grant, the reward for inventiveness and for having contributed to the technological and material interests of the nation.

Patents are only issued to an individual and not to legal entities such as a business or other organizations. The individual can assign the legal control over to a business and in many instances may be obligated to adhere to a patent waiver agreement as a pre-condition for employment. This agreement confirms that the corporation assumes legal control and use of the patent that has been registered in the name of one of its employees. Through whatever legal means that they are secured, businesses currently maintain control over 70 percent of all outstanding patents.[10]

Well over 100,000 applications are submitted to the Patent office each year and over 70,000 new patents are annually issued. On average, three years elapse between the submission of a patent application and the final determination of the Patent Office. During the period of patent review, an applicant is accorded the same legal protection as is provided once the patent is actually issued. If the product or process is produced and marketed during this period of application review, the applicant is permitted to stamp or print the statement: "Patent Pending," to demonstrate its patent intent. This effectively extends the actual length of the patent period beyond the 17 year period.

Most critics of the patent system accept the need to provide some monopoly protection as a means of providing an incentive for the uncertainty and costly risk of research and new product development. Additionally, an entering firm may be able to solidify its market position through the award of a patent and thus intensify competitive conditions within an industry. However there is growing concern over the possible abuses of the patent system. Does it provide a legally permissible way for firms to entrench their monopolistic control over markets and do patents alternatively suppress technological advance?

Unlike most other countries, the United States does not require that the patent be "worked" or actually applied. The irony is that an exclusive monopoly privilege is granted on the premise that the patented product or process is distinguishably unique and theoretically will enhance the interests of the nation. Yet, a relatively small portion, 25 to 30 percent of all outstanding patents, are typically being applied. This situation raises grave questions about the effectiveness of the patent law and adds credence to the opponents' view that they are often used to suppress technological advance. A firm might be understandably hesitant to introduce a newly patented technology or product if it resulted in the obsolescence of existing production processes or profitable markets.

Most other nations obligate holders of patents to apply them or will waive the requirement if just cause is provided. It is evident that not all new products or technologies can be profitably introduced into the marketplace. The financial risk, excessive capitalization requirements, or a limited and unprofitable market potential may be sufficient justification for companies of any size to withhold a patent. It would appear, however, that the limited portion being applied is perhaps attributable to less justifiable reasons and reflects a legally permissible decision to suppress the patent as a means of ensuring continued monopolistic dominance within an industry.

In addressing this issue, a possible solution might be that unworked patents become available to others through an open competitive bid process after so many years have elapsed. If after 4 or 5 years a patent holder has not applied the patent, then it could be assigned through a publicized bid process to someone else for application. This recommendation would provide compensation to the original holder and more importantly ensure that the legislative intent of the patent system is being met.

Rather than the presently fixed 17 year monopoly period many critics suggest that the patent life should be variable. The calculated patent privilege should be sufficient to ensure the holder of a generous profit return that is reasonably equated with the technological importance and financial risk assumed with its discovery and introduction. Should a hula-hoop or other minimal risk, unsophisticated novelties be accorded the same monopoly grant as that provided for costly and complex technological discoveries in the health or manufacturing industries?

Of equal concern is the skewed distribution of patents among relatively small and larger-sized firms. The nation's patent law does not limit the number of patents which can be controlled by a firm. Thus, within many concentrated industries, the largest share of patents is held by one or a select few dominant firms within the industry. In effect, this situation has contributed to the monopolization of patents which solidifies the dominant firms' control over its respective industry technology and markets.

Within some industries, companies may agree to pool their patents through a trade association or a company that has been solely established for this purpose. Under these pooled arrangements, industry-related patents held by individual companies become available for use by all of the participating member firms. This arrangement can possibly intensify industry competition by making comparable technology available to all of the participating companies. Alternatively, it can serve to diminish competition and entrench the ologopolistic control of its members over the market. Those firms which are not members of the pooled arrangements and do not have access to this shared technology may find this to be an unsurmountable impediment or barrier to their competitive success.

Production and distribution practices which would be declarably per se violations of the antitrust laws are permissible under various forms of patent pooling and patent licensing arrangements. A patent holder may license another firm or firms, with compensation, to use the patent under negotiated conditions. The patent license arrangement may specify to the licensee the quantities to be produced, the limited geographic markets in which the product may be distributed, and the price at which it is to be sold.

An additional issue relates to the basic question of what constitutes patentability. It is evident that the framers of the law intended this exceptional monopoly privilege to be extended for exceptional and unquestioned "strokes of genius." What constitutes such a definitional discovery or product remains very much in doubt and erodes the basic integrity and justification of the patent law. Much has been written about the unmanageably large number of patent applications submitted each year and the questioned qualifications of the staff examiners to evaluate the diverse complexity of advanced technology. It is clear that patents are often issued for many things that do not fulfill the definitional qualities implied in the law. Indeed, in a judicial proceeding involving infringement, the Patent Office will not attest to the unique patentability of the patent which it had earlier granted. When contested, the burden of justifying a granted patent rests upon the individual party. In these instances, the court must interpretatively decide the technological differences or variances in product quality or function among the parties. Ultimately, the question of patentability rests upon the judgment of the courts.

In many cases, the courts have consistently upheld the legality of the patent waiver agreement as a pre-requisite to employment and the right of a company to dictate production, distribution, and pricing strategies to a licensee under patent license arrangements. One area in which the courts have aggressively prosecuted involves an abusive effort among firms to extend the permissible scope of their patent privilege. Efforts among firms to include tying contracts into their patent licensing agreements or to obligate a lesee of their patented products to buy other company products has been condemned by the courts. The courts decreed that the RCA Company violated the permissible bounds of its patent privilege when it contractually obligated its licensed manufacturers of RCA radios to equally buy RCA tubes.[11] Equally, the court ruled against the IBM Corporation for requiring the lessees of patented IBM hardware to buy tabulating cards from IBM. [12]

SUMMARY:

The statutes discussed in this chapter represent a striking departure from the legislative intent and spirit of the antitrust laws. Rather than promoting a competitive market environment, they tend to diminish competitive intensity and promote or entrench monopolistic elements within the economy. Without exception, these inconsistent legislative acts constitute a response to a perceived economic need to enhance the export competitiveness of the smaller-sized firms, to preserve the survival of the marginal retail businesses, or to ensure continued technological and innovative advances. In each instance, it was assumed that the nation's economic interests were being best served and that the cost of inconsistency was outweighed by the longer-term benefits to the recipient businesses and the economy as a whole. While the interpretative costs versus benefits of this policy direction are difficult to quantify, it is clear that they undermine the supportive justification for pursuing a regulatory policy. The impact of a policy which seeks to competitively insulate one business against another may not simultaneously ensure the interests of the consuming population. Ultimately, it is the welfare of the consumer, the entire population, which most critically justifies governmental intervention and the imposition of regulatory restraints and policy.

FOOTNOTES

Table 1 - Source: Data for Table has been calculated from FTC mimeographed publication entitled: Alphabetical List of Firms, Organizations and Individuals Registering Under The Webb-Pomerene Act between April, 1918 and May, 1965, and the yearly listings of Webb Associations and their participating members. Classifications of industries was based upon concentration ratios published in Bureau of Census, Concentration Ratios in Manufacturing Industries, 1966.

1. U.S. Senate Foreign Trade Subcommittee, Small Business and the Webb-Pomerene Act, (U.S. Government Printing Office, Washington, D.C.), 1946, p.4.

2. Business America, publication of the U.S. Department of Commerce, Washington, D.C., October 18, 1982, p.4.

3. Richard Caves, American Industry: Structure, Conduct, Performance, 3rd Ed., Prentice-Hall, Inc., Englewood Cliffs, N.J., 1972, p.82.

4. Federal Trade Commission v. Anheuser-Busch, Inc., 363 U.S. 536 (1960).

5. Eugene M. Singer, Antitrust Economics and Legal Analysis, Grid Publishing Co., Columbus, Ohio, 1981, p.120.

6. Corn Products Refining Co. v. FTC 324 U.S. 726 (1945).

7. Sun Oil Co. v. Federal Trade Commission, 371 U.S. 505 (1963).

8. Ibid, p.125.

9. Federal Trade Commission v. Morton Salt Co., 334 U.S. 37 (1948).

10. William C. Shepard and Clair Wilcox, Public Policies Toward Business, 6th Edition, Richard D. Irwin, Inc., 1979, p.501.

11. Lord v.Radio Corporation of America, 24 F. 2d 505 (1928). This case is discussed in Shepard and Wilcox, p.513.

12. Ibid., p.513.

CHAPTER READINGS

Bork, R.H., The Antitrust Paradox: A Policy at War with Itself. Basic Books, New York, 1978.

Caves, Richard, Amerian Industry: Structure, Conduct, Performance, 3rd Ed. Prentice-Hall, Inc., Englewood Cliffs, N.J. 1972.

Gellhorn, E. Antitrust Law and Economics, West Publishing Co., St. Paul, 1976, Chap. 2,3.

Posner, R.A., Antitrust Law, University of Chicago Press, Chicago Illinois, 1976, Chap. 5-8.

Stelzer, I.M., Selected Antitrust Cases, Richard D. Irwin, Homewood, Illinois, 1976.

Shepard, William and Wilcox, Clair, Public Policies Toward Business, Richard D. Irwin, Homewood, Illinois, 1979.

Singer, Eugene, Antitrust Economics and Legal Analysis, Grid Publishing Co., Columbus, Ohio, 1981.

CHAPTER FIVE

MERGERS AND ACQUISITIONS

Mergers and consolidations have always assumed a prominent role in the economic history of the nation. The first evident wave of acquisitions occurred during the early stages of the industrial revolution and culminated in a substantial level of absolute and relative size concentration by 1910. The Sherman Antitrust Act represented a legislative response to many abusive market practices, but was largely precipitated by the alarming growth in trusts and other forms of consolidations.

While the incidence of merger activity has varied over the years, they have more recently assumed recognized prominence because of their volume and increased unprosecutable nature. Recall, that the Sec. 3 provision of the Clayton Act prohibits mergers through stock acquisition if it provingly results in a substantial lessening of competition. Businesses readily circumvented the prosecutable thrust of the Clayton Act by arranging mergers through the acquisition of assets. This loop-hole was closed in 1950 with the enactment of the Celler-Kefauver Act which amended Sec. 7 by prohibiting those acquisitions consummated through asset purchase which contributed to an illegal lessening of competition and monopoly growth.

In an effort to provide greater clarification and enhance merger decision-making among businesses, the Congress enacted the Hart-Scott-Rodino Antitrust Improvements Act in 1976. This statute obligates dominant large-sized companies to notify the Justice Department of their intentions to pursue a merger. Specifically, the Act amended Sec. 7 of the Clayton Act and obligates certain companies which seek to consolidate to advise the Antitrust Division of their merger intentions at least thirty days in advance. This pre-notification requirement applied to those companies with respective assets or sales of 100 million and 10 million or more respectively. Thus, if company A with assets of over 100 million seeks to consolidate with company B which has annual sales of over 10 million, they are legally bound to advise the antitrust authorities of their merger interests. This pre-merger notification policy provides a level of direction to businesses and serves the additional benefit of permitting the antitrust officials to assume legal action before a merger is actually finalized.

DIFFERENT TYPES OF MERGERS:

There are three basic ard recognized forms of mergers. They are:

(1) Horizontal Mergers which involve a consolidation of firms which are producing and/or distributing related and substitutable products and services. This type of merger involves firms that are rivals and most typically competing among each other within the same industry. A merger between the Hertz and Avis car rental companies or Spalding and Wilson Sporting Goods companies would be examples of a horizontal merger. The impact of a horizontal merger upon market conditions within that industry whether it intensifies or diminishes competition, can be most readily quantified and determined by the courts.

(2) Vertical Mergers involve companies that are typically in a supplier-manufacturer relationship. However, although they involve companies that are producing or generating different products and/or services in distinctly different markets, they compliment each other's business operations through the interaction of supplier of resource inputs in the processing and distribution of a finished product of service. A consolidation between the General Tire Company and American Motors Corp. would be an example of a vertical merger.

(3) Conglomerate Mergers assume varied forms but most typically apply to consolidations among firms that are producing or generating unrelated and distinguishably different products and/or services. A merger between IBM and the Appalachian Coal Mining Company or General Motors and a meat-packing company would be examples of a conglomerate merger. Mergers may be additionally categorized as market or product-extension in nature. A consolidation involving market-extension would be one in which a regional producer of hats merges with another hat manufacturer in a different region of the country. Those firms are producing similar products in different territorial markets with the merger now extending the firm's geographic market coverage. Alternatively, a product-extension merger solidifies a firm's market control over different, but related products. A manufacturer of breakfast cereals may merge with a manufacturer of frozen waffles or pancakes as a means of extending the company's diversified control over this broadly related market.

Perhaps no merger related term has become more recognizable in recent years than that of "conglomerates". It relates to those firms, initially single-product based, which have diversified into multi-product lines through merger activity. While many of these companies have been successful and have become the biggest within the economy, the initial fascination which they attracted has diminished.

THE IMPETUS TO MERGE:

Businesses that initiate mergers are motivated by many diverse conditions. One historic and compelling incentive has been the interest in diversifying a firm's product lines. Product diversification can minimize risk equated within single line production, most evident among primary defense-related manufacturers whose business will erratically fluctuate in response to often unpredictable changes in the nation's defense spending. Equally, it can serve to compliment a firm's primary business lines or enable a firm to enter a new and evolving market that may have great future potential. Product diversity, particularly if it is scientifically or technologically related to primary product lines can be a very wise and profitable business strategy. Equally, it may contribute to a firm's competitive posture and intensify competition within the diverse markets that are impacted by the merger.

A consolidation may be economically feasible if it results in accrued economies to scale which lower incremental production and/or distribution costs. A horizontal merger among two relatively small producers may contribute to substantial cost reductions through volume resource purchases, economies of increased plant production, or distribution cost savings in product promotion or transportation. These lesser operating costs may strengthen the market position of the merged business and further the overall incidence of competition within the industry. Equally, a vertical merger might provide a smaller manufacturer with the needed cost advantages associated with the ownership of a supplier subsidiary to ensure its competitive success within its industry.

In sum, mergers can be readily justified and encouraged as a positive means of strengthening competition within the economy. The measured benefits of potential cost-reductions and market-creation opportunities particularly among the smaller-sized firms within an industry are economically sound justification for mergers.

Less credible incentives for mergers may reflect a firm's interest in minimizing industry competition through the acquisition of a competitor. A horizontal merger among larger firms within an industry which individually have entrenched their market position is difficult to justify and would likely be declared illegal under the antitrust laws. Its been increasingly observed, that many mergers are initiated solely to satisfy the driven interests of a chief executive to amass a dominant and recognizable industrial empire. Existing large dominant-sized firms which continue to aggressively initiate "take-overs" may be more motivated by the quest to achieve a multi-billion dollar industrial giant than the justifiable need to accrue added productive, distributive, or technological economies which would enhance the firm's competitive position. This incentive to merge can be least justified since it fails to favorably effect productive-capacity or competitive cost conditions.

Becoming a larger-sized business through merger acquisitions does not necessarily ensure greater profitability through incurred economies to scale. Many studies have confirmed that the profit performance of merged companies has been significantly inferior to the financial success experienced by smaller-sized firms which have enjoyed internal market growth.[1]

THE COMPOSITION OF MERGERS:

There has been a very substantial change in the composition of mergers during the past several decades. Considering the enforcement loop-hole contained in the Clayton Act, it is not surprising that horizontal mergers historically comprised the largest share of all consolidation activity. As the data in Table I indicates, the 1950 amendment embodied in the Celler-Kefauver Act increased the effectiveness of merger prosecution. The enactment of the Celler Act singularily accounted for the precipitous decline in horizontal mergers and the sharp rise in conglomerate acquisitions comprised 27.6 percent, horizontal mergers 67.6 percent, and vertical mergers 4.8 percent of all acquisition activity between 1926 and 1930. Horizontal mergers sharply declined from that relative high to comprise a limited 7.7 percent during the decade of the 60's. In sharp contrast, conglomerate mergers have represented a larger and larger share of merger activity and accounted for over 81.6 percent of all acquisitions during the period between 1966 and 1968. More recently, its now estimated that conglomerate mergers comprise well over 91 percent of all acquisitions.

Table 1

Composition of Mergers of Types (1926-1968)

Merger Type	1930	1947	1955	1960	1965	1968
Horizontal	67.2	62.0	35.1	22.7	16.4	7.7
Vertical	4.8	17.0	12.2	14.9	17.5	9.8
Conglomerate	27.6	21.0	52.7	62.4	66.1	82.5
(a) Product Extension	19.3	21.0	48.6	55.0	60.0	81.6
(b) Market Extension	8.3	-	4.1	7.4	6.1	0.9

Several reasons explain the dramatic change in the composition of merger activity over the past thirty years. It does reflect the popularized interests of business to diversify their product lines but is more likely attributable to the greater susceptibleness of horizontal mergers to antitrust prosecution. Since it involves a consolidation among formerly competing firms within the same industry, it is relatively easy to quantify the impact of the merger on concentration and the structural characteristics of the industry. Thus, if the consolidation is found to contribute to an excessive level of market dominance, the courts have moved swiftly to block, or if necessary, negate the firm's merger interest.

In contrast, it is often more difficult to quantify the impact of conglomerate acquisitions on market power. It is difficult to empirically evaluate the market effects of a merger among firms servicing different markets and producing unrelated products. Yet, to be prosecuted and interpretatively found in violation of the law requires confirmation that there has been a "substantial lessening of competition" within the industry. Recall the earlier noted distinction between absolute-size and relative-size concentration. Conglomerate mergers do measurably increase the absolute size of a firm and have importantly contributed to the increased share of total manufacturing assets and sales attributable to a select few large-sized corporations. This measure of firm size is not illegal and is not subject to prosecution under present antitrust standards. In contrast, it is difficult, and often impossible, to evaluate the impact of a conglomerate merger upon relative-size concentration. While the acquisition has increased the asset and annual sales size of the acquiring company (absolute size), it may not have impacted upon its market share within those distinctly different mergered product markets. Since relative-size concentration remains the only prosecutable standard, these mergers have not been effectively prosecuted.

The added concern of regulatory officials relates to the large share of total merger activity attributable to the initiative of relatively large-sized companies.[2] Thus, mergers have and continue to inflate the overall levels of concentration within manufacturing and have substantially skewed the size distribution of firms within most sectors of the national economy. The initial wave of merger activity at the end of the 19th century transformed the economy from its relative atomistic competitive characteristics to an increasingly concentrated and monopolistic structured framework. This process has become increasingly complete with continued merger activity through the 20th century.

The subcommittee report concluded:

> "...mergers have been an important force in concentrating industrial assets in the hands of a few very large corporations and it is no mere coincidence that the only periods in which the largest corporations sharply increased their share of overall manufacturing activity were those of extensive merger activity." [3]

The incidence of merger activity among the large-sized corporations has become more pronounced in this decade. Recent mergers among existing large dominant competing firms in the steel and petroleum industries are representative examples of the continued impact of consolidation activity upon the structural characteristics of the nation's economy.

INTERNATIONAL MERGER ACTIVITY:

Consolidation activity has not been confined to domestic firms. Through direct investment, the acquisition of foreign based businesses has assumed significant proportions and constitutes an issue of controversial importance for many foreign governments. International merger activity has been initiated by businesses seeking to penetrate foreign markets or to achieve productive and distributive economies in meeting both foreign and domestic market demands. It has been reported that the composition of international mergers between 1965 and 1972 consisted notably of horizontal acquisitions which comprised 84 percent of the total, vertical mergers totalled 4 percent, and conglomerate mergers 12 percent.[4]

Table II

Mergers and Acquisitions in the Canadian Economy (1960-1973)

Year	Total Mergers	Domestic	Foreign	Foreign to Domestic (%)
1960	203	110	93	46*
1961	238	152	86	36
1962	185	106	79	43
1963	129	88	41	32
1964	204	124	80	39
1965	235	157	78	33
1966	203	123	80	39
1967	228	143	85	37
1968	402	239	163	41
1969	504	336	168	86
1970	427	265	162	39
1971	388	245	143	37
1972	429	302	127	30
1973	352	252	100	28

The data in Table II illustrates the volume and composition of mergers, initiated by domestic or international based companies in the Canadian economy during the period from 1960 to 1973. International mergers have constituted a large share of total acquisitions within the nation's manufacturing sector, ranging from a high of 46 percent in 1960 to 28 percent in 1973. For a long period in Canada's economic history, the nation has encouraged foreign direct investment through the introduction of various business incentives, most notably a favorable protectionist policy to insulate domestic based manufacturers against foreign competitors. More recently however, Canadian government officials have become concerned with their domestic economy. Through international mergers, over 40 percent of the entire manufacturing sector is owned or controlled by U.S. business interests, and within specific industries (autos, steel, rubber, etc.), the share of ownership is significantly higher. The Canadian government has recently responded with legislation which establishes an upper limit to the portion of industry ownership and control that can be foreign based. This example is reasonably representative of the importance of international merger activity within many other industrialized nations throughout the world.

MERGER GUIDELINES:

A large number of mergers, totaling well over 200,000 annually, has recently characterized the domestic economy. However, the wave of acquisitions during the decade of the 60's was atypically high, both in total number and in the value of acquired assets and sales volume. It has and continues to be evident that the Justice Department has insufficient resources to challenge every questionable acquisition and thus has pursued a policy of selective prosecution. This selective policy was intended to establish important precedence but equally contributed to risky uncertainty for businesses that were contemplating a merger initiative. If they proceeded to finalize a merger, would it invite prosecution? To minimize this uncertainty and to assist businesses in arriving at some knowing sense of self-determination, the Justice Department first announced a set of guidelines in 1968 which were substantially revised in 1982. These guidelines were not intended to be absolute, but rather provided an interpretative guide for businesses in anticipating the probable course of action that the Justice Department would pursue. The guidelines, issued in 1968, provide the following evaluative standards for horizontal, vertical and conglomerate mergers.

(1) Horizontal Mergers:

(a) If the four firm concentration ratio is 75 percent or more, the Justice Department announced that it would likely challenge an intended merger among firms within that industry that have the following market shares:

Acquiring Firm	Acquired Firm
4%	4% or more
10%	2% or more
15%	1% or more

(b) If the four firm concentration ratio is 75 percent or less, the Justice Department announced that it would likely challenge an intended merger among firms within that industry that have the following market shares:

Acquiring Firm	Acquired Firm
5%	5% or more
10%	4% or more
15%	3% or more
20%	2% or more
25%	1% or more

In addition, any merger among firms within the same industry that have respective market shares of over 2 percent would be challenged if there is substantial evidence that overall concentration has been increasing within the industry. A likely exception to this norm would involve a company that has not prospered and would likely terminate activity within the industry if a merger could result in its revitalized market health.

(2) Vertical Mergers:

(a) Any consolidation among suppliers and manufacturers that would provingly diminish competition and contribute to prohibitively high barriers to entry would be challenged. The standard applied to vertical mergers centers around the so-called 6-10 rule. A merger will be challenged if the supplier accounts for 10 percent or more of its market sales and the purchaser (manufacturer of final products) has a respective market share of 6 percent or more. The respective market shares of the two firms assumes that a merger which conforms to this empirical norm would erect unsurmountably high barriers to entry. If the evidence does not support this barrier expectation, the merger might not be prosecuted by the Justice Department.

(b) A proposed merger involving a purchaser (manufacturer) with a market share of 10 percent or more and a supplying company whose market share may be less than 6 percent but who accounts for 20 percent or more of the supplier purchases of the manufacturer may be challenged. Of importance in judging the probable response of the Justice Department to vertical mergers is the trends in economic concentration within the respective industries and the estimated effect of the acquisition upon barriers to entry.

(3) Conglomerate Mergers:

The very nature of conglomerate mergers makes the establishment of equally definitive and empirically expressed standards more difficult. In sum, the guidelines have accentuated the probable impact of such a merger on reciprocity results and barriers to entry. In sum, an acquisition may be challenged if a dominant firm within an industry merges with a company that has the strong potential of successfully entering that industry. Or, a merger which may contribute to excessive reciprocity arrangements may be equally challenged. Adjusted slightly in 1969 and 1970, the guidelines further specify that a conglomerate merger is susceptible to litigation if it involves any of the 200 largest industrial firms with a firm whose asset value approximates or exceeds 100 million. Additionally, a consolidation initiated by one of the 200 largest corporations with a firm that has a relative market share of 10 percent or more will be potentially challenged.

1982 MERGER GUIDELINES:

The Justice Department's announced new guidelines in 1982 philosophically reflect the view that mergers are healthy to the nation's economy and should not be prohibited unless the larger merged company exhibits unacceptable monopolistic behavior. In general, these guidelines permit the consummation of many horizontal-type mergers that would have been challenged under the former evaluative standards. The revision represents more permissive acceptance of increased economic concentration and entails more complex and calculated analysis than that required under the former guidelines. They apply almost singularly to horizontal mergers and ensure that both vertical and conglomerate acquisitions will be uncontested unless there is substantial evidence of erected barriers-to-entry or increased reciprocity behavior.

Recall that the evaluative emphasis under the former guidelines was upon the four firm concentration ratio. Notably, if it exceeded 75 percent, the industry was considered highly concentrated and few mergers would have been tolerated under these market conditions. In contrast, the present standards employ a new technique for measuring economic concentration. Named the Herfindahl Index, it is derived by squaring the market shares of each firm within the industry and then summing the calculated values. If the summed value of the squared market shares for all industry firms is less than 1,000 the industry is considered to be unconcentrated, and any mergers among the firms is not likely to be challenged. The new guideline identifies a moderately concentrated industry as one in which the summed squared market shares of all the firms is within a range of 1,000 to 1,800. Within these definitional bounds, a merger among industry firms will be challenged only if it has the effect of increasing the index by 100 points or more. Under the former guidelines, two firms with respective market shares of 7 and 6 percent would be challenged if they sought to merge, since moderate concentration would imply an industry in which the four firm concentration ratio is 75 percent or less. Under the present standards, however, the squared summed value of their individual market shares is 85 points ($7^2+6^2=85$), less than the prescribed minimum of 100, and the merger would be unchallenged. Lastly, highly concentrated industries are ones in which the Herfindahl Index exceeds 1,800. Within these industries, a merger would be uncontested if it contributed an additional 50 points or more to the overall industry point value. If two firms with respective market shares of 5 and 5 percent sought to merge, the acquisition would have been challenged under the former standards since a highly concentrated industry definitely meant a four firm concentration ratio of 75 percent or more. However, under the revised guidelines, the squared summed value of their individual market shares is 41 points ($5^2 + 4^2 = 41$), less than the prescribed minimum of 50, and the merger would be unchallenged.

A comparison between both methods can be made from the information which appears in Table III (pg. 88). Note that the four firm concentration ratio among the four largest firms is 50 percent, which indicates a moderately concentrated industry. It is likely that if firms number 5 and 6 sought to merge, it would result in the merged corporation having a market share of 15 percent, which would rival that of the dominant number 1 firm. Without certainty, it seems probable that this merger might have been challenged under the former guidelines. Under the present standards, the summed value of each firm's squared market share is only 860 points. Below the definable norm of 1,000 points, this industry is considered unconcentrated and mergers among firms are not very susceptible to prosecution. It is evident that many mergers that might formerly have been subject to litigation will be uncontested under the new guidelines and that overall concentration will increase.

Table III

Contrasting Measures of Economic Concentration

Company		Market Share old Method	Herfindahl Method (share squared)
1		15%	225 pt.
2		15%	196 pt.
3		12%	144 pt.
4		9%	81 pt.
5		8%	64 pt.
6		7%	49 pt.
7		6%	36 pt.
8		5%	25 pt.
Others		24%	Est. 40 pt.
	Total	100%	Total 860 pt.

MERGERS AND THE COURTS:

The potential illegality of merger activity under the Clayton and Celler Acts rests critically upon the judicial interpretation of the relevant product and relevant geographical markets. Whether the products of the consolidated companies were formerly substitutable or distinctly different will determine the court's assessment of the merger upon market competition. Equally, the territorial bounds of the market which may have been affected by the merger critically determine the judicial decision regarding market power and economic concentration.

During litigation, the antitrust officials will urge the court to accept a narrow interpretation of the relevant geographical market whereas the companies will press for a broad interpretation as a means of minimizing the calculated effects of the merger upon market competition.

PHILADELPHIA COMMERCIAL BANK CASE:

In The United States v. Philadelphia National Bank, the case involved a proposed merger among two commercial banks that were serving the Philadelphia metropolitan area. The regulatory officials urged that the relevant geographical market be narrowly defined to encompass notably the metropolitan Philadelphia area. Under this limiting definition of the market boundaries, it was determined that the merged bank would have a market share of over 30 percent of all the commercial banking business. Considered excessive, the court was urged to judge this merger illegal under the provision of the Celler-Kefauver Act.[5]

In contrast, the banks argued that the Relevant Geographical Market should be more broadly defined to include the Northeastern corridor bounded by Metropolitan New York and Philadelphia. The banks sought the broader definition to demonstrate the benefitting results of the merger which would enhance its ability to effectively compete with the larger commercial banks in the New York area. Equally, a broad definition of the market would have substantially lessened its estimated market share to less than 3 percent. Finally decided by the Supreme Court, the decision emphasized the narrow interpretation of the geographical market. The court ruled that the consolidation would be a violation of the law since a merged market share of over 30 percent within the limited Philadelphia area was excessive.

VON GROCERY CASE:

Another example of a horizontal merger involved the consolidation of two retail food chain stores that were serving the metropolitan Los Angeles area.[6] In 1958, the Von's Grocery Company, the third largest food chain with a market share of 4.7 percent acquired the Shopping Bag Company, the 6th largest, with a market share of 2.8 percent. The company argued that its merged market share within metropolitan Los Angeles area was only 7.5 percent and that the interpretative bounds of the territorial market extended beyond the immediate L.A. area. In reversing the lower court's decision, the Supreme Court ruled that this merger was a violation of the law. Interestingly, the merged market share was only 7.5 percent, but the Court emphasized the industry trends within the limited and narrow market area. The Court was concerned that the number of small grocery store competitors had declined substantially within the market and that both companies had prospered and increased its number of retail outlets independently before the merger. Thus, this consolidation was not needed to ensure their market survival and only served to increase the level of industry concentration.

THE CONTINENTAL CAN COMPANY CASE:

In United States v. Continental Can Company, the judicial decision centered around an interpretation of the relevant product market.[7] The Continental Can Company was the nation's second largest manufacturer of metal cans with an estimated market share of 33 percent. The Hazel-Atlas Company was the third largest producer of glass containers with a market share of 9.6 percent. The Continental Can Company acquired the Hazel-Atlas Glass Company through the purchase of its stock for the expressed purpose of diversifying its related product lines. Initially, a district court upheld this acquisition, ruling that this involved a product-extension conglomerate merger among firms producing related, but distinctly different products. Upon appeal, the Supreme Court reversed the lower court decision. The Court held that metal and glass containers were different but that their functional uses were sufficiently related and substitutable to constitute a single product market. This narrow interpretation of the relevant product market meant that the merger contributed to excessive monopoly power within a limited defined market and was in violation of the law.

BROWN SHOE COMPANY CASE:

A case decided upon a judicial interpretation of both the relevant geographical and product markets involved a merger between two producers and distributors of shoes. [8] The antitrust officials brought suit under the Celler-Kefauver Act to block the Brown Shoe Company's merger initiative with the G.R. Kinney Company. Prior to the merger, the Brown Shoe Company was the third largest retailer with an estimated 2.1 percent of all retail outlets and accounted for a market share of 4.0 percent of total industry sales. The Kinney Company was the 8th largest retailer, with 1.5 percent of all industry sales outlets and a manufacturing market share of 0.5 percent. The Justice Department's suit centered upon the horizontal implications of the merged retail outlets and the additional vertical integration that would be strengthened by the manufacturer-retail relationships of the two companies.

The company sought a broad interpretation of the relevant product market and the relevant geographical market. It argued that the product market should encompass all shoe production and distribution within the broad territorial bounds of the national market. In contrast, the Justice Department advanced the position that the relevant product market should be narrowly defined to reflect differences in product prices among three distinct categories of men's, women's, and children's shoes. Additionally, it argued that the relevant geographical market should be more narrowly defined to include those market areas with a resident population of ten thousand or more. In accepting the more narrow definition of the market, the Court then evaluated the impact of the merger among the three distinct and separable product markets. Even though the merged firm accounted for only 4 percent of all retail outlets within the industry, the Supreme Court ruled that its product shares of women's, men's, and children's shoes within the limited definition of the geographical markets would be excessive. Brown was ordered to divest its ownership interest in the Kinney Company as a result of this judicial decision.

Unlike horizontal mergers where judicial emphasis is centered upon the "lessening of competition" effects of the consolidation, vertical mergers emphasize the potential "restraint upon competitors" and the potential cost efficiencies that may accrue from integration.

GENERAL MOTORS AND DUPONT MERGER:

Among the most celebrated vertical merger cases involved the General Motors and DuPont Corporations.[9] The DuPont Corporation, a dominant manufacturer of chemicals, paints, and fabrics had acquired a 23 percent share of G.M. stock over a period of many years. As a major supplier to the automotive industry, the Justice Department charged that this equity holding violated the Section 7 provision of the Clayton Act since it would impede the competitive position of other suppliers within the industry. The DuPont Company argued that the relevant product market should be broadly defined to include all types of finishes and fabrics, whereas the antitrust officials successfully argued that the product market limitedly encompassed those distinct products that were manufactured almost exclusively for the automotive industry. The Court accepted the narrow product market interpretation and additionally considered the individual dominance of both firms within their respective markets. The company was found to have violated the merger provision of the Clayton Act and was ordered to divest its holding of G.M. stock.

Conglomerate mergers are much less susceptible to antitrust prosecution than are horizontal or vertical consolidations. It is often very difficult to document the impact of a conglomerate merger upon "the lessening of competition" within a definable product market or to assess the result of the consolidation upon competitors within an industry. Thus, in instances in which the regulatory officials have initiated legal proceedings against conglomerate mergers, the emphasis has been upon the "elimination of potential competitors" or that the acquiring firm may entrench the dominant position of its merged firm through varied forms of financial subsidization or reciprocity arrangements.

THE PROCTOR AND GAMBLE CASE:

In 1967, the Proctor and Gamble Company merged with the Clorox Company which was the nation's largest manufacturer of household liquid bleach.[10] Proctor and Gamble was a leading manufacturer of soap and detergent products and its products had achieved substantial differentiation within their markets. The Clorox Company had equally enjoyed significant success and accounted for a market share of 48.8 percent of total industry sales. Its nearest competitors had respective market shares of 15.7 and 5.9 percent and the remaining portion of the market was distributed among an additional 200 relatively small-sizes firms. A lower court initially decreed that the merger was not permissible since the Proctor and Gamble Company could not have independently entered the household bleach market. Upon appeal, the Supreme Court reversed this earlier decision and ordered the companies to disengage from the merger.

Of importance in the Court's decision was the relative dominance of both companies within their respective product markets, and the absence of substantial technological or financial bariers-to-entry within the household bleach industry. The Court argued that Proctor and Gamble possessed the financial and technological resources to penetrate this industry without the need to eliminate a potential competitor. The Court stated:

> "...the substitution of the powerful acquiring firm for the smaller, but already dominant firm may substantially reduce the competitive structure of the industry by raising entry barriers and by dissuading the smaller firms from aggressively competing." [11]

THE BLACK AND DECKER CASE:

The Justice Department sought unsuccessfully to use this similar "potential competitor" argument in a merger involving the Black and Decker and McCulloch companies in 1976. The Black and Decker Company, a leading manufacturer of electrical tools, merged with the McCulloch Company, a leading manufacturer of gasoline powered chain saws. While the product lines of the two companies is distinctly different, the antitrust officials argued that the Black and Decker Company had the necessary resources to successfully enter the chainsaw industry. The Court rejected this argument since electric and gas powered products were distinguishably different and required unique technological expertise. Additionally, the Court rejected the argument that the merger among these dominant firms would entrench and solidify McCulloch's position within its industry. The Court permitted this merger since several of McCulloch's direct competitors had equally strong or greater financial and sales success within the industry. [12]

Another defense often advanced to justify a merger relates to the rejuvenated competitive strength that a weak or failing company accrues through consolidation with a growing and healthy firm. This "failing firm" thesis was successfully advanced in the U.S. v. General Dynamics Corporation case. [13] The General Dynamics Corporation acquired the Material Service Corporation which owned several coal mining companies. This merger made the General Dynamics Corporation the fifth largest coal producer in the country. The Justice Department sought to block the merger, arguing that the consolidation would further the trend towards greaer concentration as more of the smaller competitors withdrew from the industry. Alternatively, the company's defense centered around the "failing firm" thesis which emphasized the benefit to competition which would result from a rejuvenated firm. The company argued that its coal reserves were rapidly being depleted and that it lacked the individual resources to remain competitive within the industry. The court accepted this defense and ruled that the merger was permissible since the acquired company lacked the resources to remain a viable competitor itself.

SUMMARY:

A dominant market position attributable to internal growth has remained relatively immune from antitrust prosecution. The firm has "met the market test," and has deservedly achieved its prominent position because of its superiority in product development, customer service, or competitive cost conditions. Under these circumstances, the rule of reason interpretation has rather consistently been applied and examples of market dominance will remain permissible as long as there is no recordable evidence of predatory or abusive market behavior.

Alternatively, market power achieved through external growth, initiated by merger and acquisition activity, is much more susceptible to antitrust litigation. Its legality is then determined by the judicial interpretation of its effects upon industry competition or its impact upon the competitive posture of rival firms. The judicial outcome is not always predictable but will interpretatively vary in accordance with the distinct circumstances of the case. The "failing firm" or "potential entrant" defense, relate the need for interpretative adaptableness to ensure that the competitive interests of the nation's economy are preserved.

FOOTNOTES

1. The results of a large number of statistical studies are summarized in: U.S. Committee on the Judiciary, Subcommittee on Antitrust and Monopoly, Economic Concentration: Economic Report on Corporate Mergers, Part 8A, 91st Cong. 1st session, U.S. Government Printing Office, Washington, D.C. 1969, pp. 100-109.

Table I - Source: Information appears in U.S. Committee on the Judiciary, Subcommittee on Antitrust and Monopoly, Economic Concentration: Economic Report on Corporate Mergers, Part 8A, 91st

Cong., 1st Session, U.S. Government Printing Office, Washington, D.C., 1969, p. 63.

2. A detailed summary of merger activity among firms of varied size in manufacturing during the period between 1948-1968 can be found in Ibid., Economic Report on Corporate Mergers, pp. 39-59.

3. Ibid., Economic Report on Corporate Mergers, p. 178.

4. Organization for Economic Co-operation and Development, Mergers and Competition Policy, Paris, France, 1974, p. 51.

Table II - Source: Organization for Economic Co-operation and Development, Mergers and Competition Policy, Paris, France, 1974, p. 48.

5. *United States* v. *Philadelphia National Bank*, 374 U.S. 321 (1963).

6. *United States* v. *Von's Grocery Company*, 384 U.S. 270 (1966).

7. *United States* v. *Continental Can Company*, 378 U.S. 441 (1964).

8. *Brown Shoe Company* v. *United States*, 370 U.S. 294 (1962).

9. *United States* v. *DuPont de Nemours and Company*, 353 U.S. 586 (1957).

10. *Federal Trade Commission* v. *The Proctor and Gamble Co.*, 386 U.S. 586 (1967).

11. Singer, pp. 153

12. A complete discussion on the "entrenchment" and "potential competitor" arguments in this case can be found in Singer, p. 15.

13. *U.S.* v. *General Dynamics Corporation*, 415 U.S. 486 (1974).

CHAPTER READINGS

Blair, John *Economic Concentration: Structure, Behavior and Public Policy*, Harcourt Brace Jovanovich, Inc., New York, 1972.

Greer, Douglas F., *Industrial Organization and Public Policy*, MacMillan Publishing Co., New York, 1980.

Organization for Economic Co-operation and Development, *Mergers and Competition Policy*, Paris, 1974.

U.S. Senate Committee on the Judiciary, Subcommittee on Antitrust and Monopoly, *Economic Concentration: Economic Report on Corporate Mergers*, Part 8A, 91st Congress, 1st Session, U.S. Government Printing Office, Washington, D.C. 1969.

Whitman, Douglas and Gergacz, John, *The Legal and Social Environment of Business*, Random House, New York, 1985, Chap. 15.

CHAPTER SIX

THE ANTITRUST LAWS AND INTERNATIONAL COMMERCE

An examination of the international dimension of antitrust policy involves many complex issues. Among them is the legalistic issue of determining extraterritorial jurisdiction and the equally complex matter of differences in regulatory philosophy among nations. These differences typically represent contrasting national economic objectives which must be respected when a nation establishes and pursues its international antitrust policies.

THE GLOBAL JURISDICTION OF U.S. LAW:

Recall that the jurisdictional application of the U.S. antitrust laws, as specified in the nation's constitution extends to both interstate and international commerce. Sec. 1 of the Sherman Act declares that any practice, contract, or conspiracy which restrains trade "among the several States or with foreign nations" is illegal. In addressing the issue of monopolizing trade or commerce, Sec. 2 decrees that it is illegal if conducted "among the several States or with foreign nations." In addition, the statutory authority of the Federal Trade Commission to extend its investigative role to foreign commerce is contained in Sec. 6 (h) of the FTC Act. In part, it declares that the Commission shall "...investigate, from time to time, trade conditions in and with foreign countries where associations, combinations, or practices of manufacturers, merchants, or traders, or other countries, may affect the foreign trade of the United States..."

An additional antitrust provision is embodied in the Wilson Tariff Act of 1894. This statute was enacted as a legislative affirmation of the nation's commercial policy objectives at that time and contained an important prohibition against import buying abuses within the domestic market. Sec. 73 of the Act prohibits any collusive behavior among importers of foreign produced goods with the purposeful intent of adversely affecting the domestic market. Any contrived practice, contract, or combination among individuals or businesses engaging in import activity which contributes to the restraint of domestic commerce or unreasonable increase in market prices is illegal. The provision states:

> "Every combination, conspiracy, trust, agreement or contract is declared to be contrary to public policy, illegal, and void...when such combination, conspiracy, trust, agreement, or contract is intended to operate in restraint of lawful trade, or free competition in lawful trade or commerce, or to increase the market price in any part of the United States..."

The antitrust laws have very broad interpretative application to export and import commerce and the activities of both native and foreign individuals engaged in international business activities. U.S. citizens and businesses as well as foreigners engaged in commercial activities which impact within the domestic markets are under the nation's regulatory jurisdiction. The limiting constraint to its application is the principle of comity among nations under the scope of international law. Comity is an expression of respectful courtesy and is defined in international law as the "recognition which one nation allows within its territory to the legislative, executive, or judicial acts of another nation, having due regard both to international duty and convenience, and to the rights of its own citizens." [1] This principle recognizes that nation's often pursue diverse and different national economic objectives which may not be in philosophical harmony with each other. Thus, U.S. antitrust application is often tempered to accommodate these differences among nations as long as the compromise does not excessively jeopardize the national interests of the nation or its citizens.

APPLICABILITY OF THE LAWS:

The effect upon U.S. foreign trade and the domestic economy is the key issue which determines the applicability of U.S. law. In general, the consistency of judicial interpretation confirms the following circumstances under which the nation's antitrust laws are internationally applied.

(1) Domestic businesses or individuals engaged in export or import activities if the effect of introduced practices, agreements, or contracts contributes to the restraint of commerce or the monopolization of domestic markets. Those illegal forms of collusive behavior which have become recognizable per se violations of the Sherman Act (price-fixing, market-sharing, product of sales quotas) in addition to the illegal prohibitions contained in the Clayton Act are equally a violation of law if introduced in foreign markets. The exception would be the exemptive umbrella provided to domestic firms that form export trade associations under the Webb-Pomerene Trade Associations.

(2) Foreign based businesses or foreign nationals that engage in commercial activities within domestic U.S. markets are subject to prosecution. Thus, those practices or forms of conspiracies which are recognizable violations of law are illegal even if the foreign businesses' government either permits or condones such behavior.

One striking difference between the U.S. antitrust laws and regulatory policy pursued by many other nations (notably the Common Market nations) is the lack of declarable per se violations. Overt and predatory per se violations of law in the U.S. are not necessarily illegal within the European Economic Community because of their governments' policy of often granting exemptions for such behavior. Thus, permissible behavior pursued by foreign businesses within their own nation may be decreed illegal and vigorously prosecuted if introduced within U.S. markets. Theoretically, foreign businesses which permissibly pursue these anti-competitive forms of market behavior within their own countries or within an integrated economic region may still be subject to U.S. prosecution even if they did not directly penetrate U.S. markets. These forms of market behavior may still be subject to U.S. litigation if, while conducted abroad, they had a substantial and documented impact upon the international commerce of the United States. The latter condition is very difficult to prosecute and is typically negated by the comity principle in which the United States would be justly hesitant to intervene in an issue involving the rights of a soverign nation to establish and pursue its own policy directives.

Since the issue of legality emphasizes the impact of activity upon the foreign trade of the U.S., the questioned behavior, whether conducted among native or foreign nationals, or whether pursued domestically or abroad is of little or no importance. In all instances, the behavior is subject to U.S. antitrust prosecution and potentially illegal if it provingly contributes to the anti-competitive erosion of U.S. interstate or foreign commerce.

COURT CASES ESTABLISHING INTERNATIONAL JURISDICTION:

Even when per se violations are permitted by foreign governments among their national firms, it is illegal for a U.S. firm to consummate agreements which impact upon domestic and foreign markets. This principle of applicability was affirmed in a case involving the American Tobacco Company and several of its English competitors. The American Tobacco Company consummated market-sharing agreements with several British rivals that resulted in the division of foreign markets. Such agreements among British firms were permissible under their national regulatory laws and a

U.S. district court initially ruled that the foreign firms had not violated U.S. law. This decision rested primarily on the premise that the foreign firms did not sell in the U.S. since the terms of the agreement designated its American rival to be the sole supplier within its domestic market. The Supreme Court later reversed this earlier decision and found that all of the companies were in violation of Sec. 1 of the Sherman Act. These British based companies, not engaged directly in trade within the U.S. market, were found guilty since the effect of the illegal agreement was judged to substantially erode the foreign trade of the nation and to additionally impede competitive conditions within the domestic market. This case further reaffirms the per se illegality of U.S. businesses participating in foreign based international cartels. Even when sanctioned by a foreign government, it is illegal for domestic firms to consummate agreements with international cartels, regardless of whether the arrangements directly impact upon the American market or exclusively upon foreign markets.

PARTICIPATION IN CARTELS:

This judicial interpretation was again re-affirmed in a case involving a cartel agreement between an American firm and its foreign competitors.[3] An American manufacturer of lead compounds finalized a market-sharing agreement with a Norwegian competitor which allocated global markets among them as a means of eliminating direct competition. Under the agreement, the U.S. market was to be supplied solely by the American firm and the Norwegian firm was the sole distributor within all other world markets, except South America. The foreign companies defense rested upon an acknowledgement of the agreement and the assumption that it was not susceptible to prosecution since it did not distribute its product within the U.S. market. The court rejected this argument and found all parties to be in violation of the Sherman Act. The Court stated:

> "The major premise of the Sherman Act is that the suppression of competition in international trade is in and of itself a public injury; or at any rate that such suppression is a greater price than we want to pay for the benefits it sometimes secures. Nor does it follow that the advance of the art, the rise in production and the decline of prices are attributable to the effects of the combination. The economic theory underlying the Sherman Act is that in the long run competition is a more effective prod to production and a more trustworthy regulator of prices than even an enlighted combination.'[4]

MONOPOLIZATION OF INTERNATIONAL MARKETS:

In addition to Sec. 1 per se violations, the Sec. 2 provision of the Sherman Act involving an effort to monopolize international trade has been judicially established. In the American Tobacco Company case, the companies were equally found to have violated Sec. 2, since the ultimate effect of their market-sharing arrangement was to solidify their monopolistic control of domestic and international markets.

A similar agreement between the General Electric Company and a dutch-based competitor to allocate the distribution of incandescent lamps within world markets was ruled in violation of both Sec. 1 and Sec. 2 of the Sherman Act.[5] In addition to restraining competitive trade within interstate and global markets, the court determined that the companies had illegally sought through these agreements to entrench and further advance their monopolistic control over their respective markets.

EXCLUSIVE DEALERSHIPS AND RECIPROCITY IN FOREIGN COMMERCE:

The prohibitive provisions of the Clayton Act regarding exclusive dealerships and tying contracts equally apply to international commerce where the determined effect is to "substantially lessen competition or tend to create a monopoly in any line of commerce". A pertinent case involved the efforts of the United Fruit Company to contractually obligate domestic buyers of its bananas to purchase all of its product needs from United Fruit Company.[6] In a consent decree, this requirement was determined to be illegal and the company was ordered to refrain from its continued use. Additionally, United Fruit was ordered to discontinue this contractual sale practice with its foreign customers when any portion of the foreign purchase was later redirected into the U.S. market. Reflecting its international applicability, it would be illegal for a foreign manufacturer to export into the U.S. market if as a condition of sale, the seller additionally obligated the domestic buyer to purchase other products or unnecessary services. Equally, a U.S. manufacturer may not contractually obligate a foreign buyer, as a condition of sale, to purchase or lease other unwanted products or unnecessary services. In both instances, the potential or documented effect of such tying arrangements upon the nation's interstate or international commerce would be legal justification for antitrust prosecution.

As earlier noted, the Sec. 6 provision of the FTC Act grants investigative authority to the Commission for purposes of determining the permissibleness of suspected conditions or firm behavior in international commerce. This jurisdictional authority was established in 1919 in a case involving the Nestle's Food Co.[7] The Commission ordered the company to discontinue its practice of placing labels on its condensed milk product which suggested that the product was being manufactured in another country. The product was actually being produced within the U.S. and the Commission's contention was that the label mislead the prospective foreign consumers as to the actual origin of the product. This was judged to be an unfair method of competition since it erroneously enhanced the foreign consumers' preference for the product at the expense of the company's competitors.

In a case involving the Eastman Kodak Co., the FTC ordered the company to discontinue the practice of coercing foreign movie producers into purchasing Kodak film as a means of insuring themselves that the company would refrain from entering the movie making industry.[8] The company appealed the Commission order on the grounds that the FTC lacked jurisdictional authority in matters involving international business agreements. Upon judicial review, the court affirmed that the FTC had proper legislative authority in such matters even though the finished product (a movie) had not yet entered the U.S. market. It was sufficient that the arrangement did involve the foreign commerce of the U.S., impacting upon foreign customers and potentially damaging domestic competitors.

INTERNATIONAL MERGERS AND ACQUISITIONS:

The earlier discussed legislation that is applied to mergers within the domestic market may be equally enforced to affect international merger activity. Similar to the issues involving the legality of firm behavior or the process of monopolization, so in issues involving equality in the matter of mergers, the judicial emphasis is centered on the evaluated effects on the U.S. market and domestic competitors.

If an American firm initiates an acquisition of a foreign competitor that is exporting into the U.S. market, the legality of the merger will be judicially comparable to the consolidation of two domestic competitors. Utilizing evaluative standards, the court will ascertain its impact upon either the relevant product market or relevant geographical market and arrive at a final judgement of legality.

Alternatively, if the acquisition involves a foreign corporation that has not penetrated the U.S. market, the judicial determination will center upon the probableness and potential of the foreign business to have entered the domestic market, independent of the merger. If the acquired foreign business had the potential to successfully penetrate the U.S. market, the question of initiating the merger to eliminate potential competition becomes judicially important. A merger that is consummated for the noted purpose of eliminating a potential foreign competitor and which may then entrench a domestic firm's monopolistic control over the U.S. market may be subject to judicial review.

Such a situation was involved in the Joseph Schlitz Company's acquisition of a foreign competitor.[9] The domestic manufacturer of beer acquired a controlling interest in the Labatt Corporation, a Canadian competitor, which was distributing its product within the domestic market through a U.S. firm which it had earlier acquired. Upon review, the court denied the acquisition since it would have eroded the potential for increased competition within the domestic market. The court determined that the American firm had achieved a successful share of the domestic market and that the acquisition of the foreign competitor would have diminished the incidence of competition within the domestic market. This ruling was based upon Labatt's ownership of a small U.S. based beer manufacturer which would have been acquired through the merger in addition to the expectation that the Canadian manufacturer could have successfully penetrated the U.S. market at any time.

It is important to note that the judicial determination is not based solely upon an immediate and documented decrease in domestic market competition. The potential impact upon competition as determined by the capability and probableness of the acquired foreign competitor to enter the domestic market is of equal judicial concern. The elimination of competition through the acquisition of a foreign competitor with a domestic market presence or the potential erosion of competition through the acquisition of a foreign manufacturer that has the resources and possible intent to enter the domestic market is subject to antitrust review. It is less likely, however, that the acquisition of a foreign competitor that has neither the resources nor the probable intent to export into the domestic market would be contested.

The acquisition of a U.S. firm, initiated by a foreign competitor, is subject to the same principle of legality. Ultimately, it is the impact of the consolidation upon domestic competition or the probable effect on industry concentration that determines its legality under the laws. In principle, a consolidation among two foreign based businesses, permissible under foreign law, may be contested under the U.S. antitrust laws if the merger has provingly impacted upon competition within the domestic markets. Efforts among U.S. regulatory officials to prosecute these mergers are necessarily constrained by the comity principle and the hesitancy of the U.S. to visibly dramatize differences in economic policy objectives among nations.

SUMMARY:

The territorial jurisdiction of the U.S. antitrust laws is global, and in principle can be applied to all forms of international commercial activities, businesses, or individuals, regardless of their national origin. The process of judicial determination regarding the legality of international activities is comparable to the standards applied to domestic economic conditions. Ultimately, the interpretative issues involving restraint of trade, the lessening of competition, or efforts to monopolize commerce, center upon the impact within domestic markets. Any transaction, practice or activity, committed among domestic or foreign businesses, whether pursued within the U.S. or abroad, is potentially illegal if it provingly erodes or restraints competition or contributes to monopolistic conditions within the American economy.

FOOTNOTES

1. Earl W. Kintner and Mark R. Joelson, *An International Antitrust Primer*, Macmillan Publishing Co., New York, 1974, p. 263.

2. *United States* v. *American Tobacco Co.*, 221 U.S. 106 (1911).

3. *United States* v. *National Lead Co.*, 332 U.S. 319 (1947).

4. Kinter and Joelson, p. 76.

5. *United States* v. *General Electric Co.*, 115 F. Supp. 835 (D.N.J. 1953).

6. *United States* v. *United Fruit Co.*, 1958 Trade Case: No. 68, 941 (E.D.La. 1958).

7. *FTC* v. *Nestle's Food Co.*, 2 F.T.C. 171 (1919).

8. *Eastman Kodak Co.* v. *FTC*, 7 F. 2d 994 (2d. Cir.1925).

9. *United States* v. *Joseph Schlitz Brewing Co.*, 385 U.S. 37 (1966).

CHAPTER READINGS

Brewster, Kingman, Jr. *Antitrust and American Business Abroad*, McGraw-Hill Book Co., Inc., New York, 1958.

Folsom, Ralph, *Corporate Competition Law in the European Communities*, Lexington Books, Lexington, Mass. 1978.

Kintner, Earl and Joelson, Mark, *An International Antitrust Primer*, MacMillan Publishing Co., New York, 1974.

Townsend, James, *Extraterritorial Antitrust in the Sherman Antitrust Act and the U.S. Business Abroad*, Westview Press, Boulder, Colorado, 1980.

CHAPTER SEVEN

AN EVALUATION OF REGULATORY POLICY

Evaluating the effectiveness of the nation's regulatory policy is difficult since its impact is interpretatively dependent upon the perspective of the individual. Certainly, its intent to ensure a competitive environment and preserve the market-oriented economy is honorable and compatible with the nation's economic and political ideals. It can certainly be stated that "having something is better than nothing" and that its overall impact upon economic conditions have been reasonably positive. The judicial acceptance of certain per se violations has insulated the consumer against certain predatory and abusive practices and has equally safeguarded the competitive position of smaller rival businesses. Equally, while the courts have retreated from the reversed rule of reason interpretation enunciated in the Alcoa case, the level of relative-size concentration would be dangerously higher than its present levels if the Sherman, Clayton, and Celler-Kefauver Acts had not been enforced. Thus, the overall effect of the antitrust legislation has been positive and it continues to exist as a graphic expression of the nation's goals and ideals.

THE WEAKNESSES OF REGULATORY POLICY:

The shortcomings and weaknesses of public policy are equally evident. Economic concentration as measured by relative-size or absolute-size standards is excessive and seriously jeopardizes the functioning and responsiveness of the market system. The incidence of a collective few large-size firms dominating their respective industry's production and distribution of product is very complete and characterizes an increasing majority of all the domestic markets. While rivalry within these industries exist, this commonly called "Workable Competition" is distinguishably different in substance and effect from that which eminates from a more stomistic structured industry. The judicial standard, summarized in the Doctrine of Conscious Parallelism, is a visible expression of the often inconsistent expectations and direction of regulatory policy. The laws' effectiveness have been weakened since judicial interpretations have not been always consistent and reaffirming. Uniformity of price, whether attributable to overt collusion or a tacit awareness among firms, is a graphic indicator of monopolistic power and market control and should become a prosecutable standard. The insertion of any interpretative dual stardard does no serve the interests of the consumer which must remain the supportable justification for enforcement.

Equally, the definitional standard of monopoly has remained legislatively and judicially elusive. What constitutes excessive relative-size and what standard should be applied to determine an illegal "lessening of competition" are critical issues. A less interpretative and more definitive standard to determine illegality under Sec. 2 of the Sherman Act or the merger provisions of the Clayton and Celler-Kefauver Act must be introduced to lessen the inconsistency of the judicial process.

This erosive inconsistency in regulatory direction is further evident in the various legislative exemptions which have been introduced through the years. The earlier initiative of individual states to enforce the price-maintenance laws, the exemptive shelter embodied in the Webb-Pomerene Act, the Patent System and others, serves to additionally erode the integrity and effectiveness of the nation's regulatory policy. Much like the judicial process, these legislative inconsistencies erect an unworkable dual standard of applicability and enforcement which further fail to serve the competitive need of the nation's economy.

Regulatory intervention is defensible and supportable if its ultimate objective is to safeguard the interests of the nation's populace. The law must always be interpreted to ensure the welfare of the consumer by insulating them from abusive market behavior. This objective is not always ensured when businesses are insulated against each other as evidenced by the fair-trade laws or some of the questioned applications of the Robinson-Patman Act provisions.

These criticisms are not intended to suggest that the nation's regulatory policy has been totally ineffective, for it has had a very positive and overall competitive-strengthening impact upon the economy. Rather, it prospective benefit will depend upon recognizing its weaknesses and seeking to legislatively introduce additional or new definitional standards of applicability.

<u>RECENT RECOMMENDED LEGISLATIVE PROPOSALS</u>:

One controversial example is the proposed Industrial Reorganization Act which was introduced for legislative discussion in 1969. Reviewed for several consecutive years by the Congress, the proposed legislation was not introduced as a perfect alternative, but rather it sought to strengthen the nation's regulatory objectives through the establishment of several new definitional standards. In sum, the legislation proposed that an illegal market condition existed if:

(1) A firm accrued a rate of return on net worth after taxes of 15 percent or more for five consecutive years,

(2) there was no evidence of substantial price competition among industry firms over three consecutive years, and

(3) the four-firm concentration ratio within an industry approximated 50 percent or more.

In essence, the initial standard would introduce absolute firm size as a potential prosecutable standard. Recall that the courts have been historically consistent in applying the antitrust laws only to relative-size concentration and have not declared bigness, itself, to be illegal. This definition is perhaps notably intended to discourage the excessive conglomerate merger activity that has remained largely immune from prosecution under the existing laws. It raises many debatable issues such as: Should a large firm, conspicuously present in diverse markets, be prosecuted because they are big? Should a firm be subject to litigation because they are successful as evidenced by their profit returns? While this new definitional norm seeks to reverse the entrenched dominance of a select few businesses, it equally introduces many complex and interpretative questions.

The second proposed standard directly addresses the Doctrine of Conscious Parallelism that characterizes oligopolistic industries. It would obligate firms to meaningfully compete on the basis of price as an expression of industry competition. Yet, as benefiting as the proposal may be, it equally raises several important issues. How is "substantial" to be determined? Must it constitute differences in price margins among the industry firms? Might it equally culminate in a market condition that it legislatively seeks to avoid? As is often defensibly advanced: would vigorous price competition be ruinous to the industry, contribute to the demise of many firms, and culminate in the survival of the competitive few? Would it then ultimately foster monopolistic growth within industries over the course of time?

Lastly, the third standard seeks to strengthen the historical use of relative-size concentration as a prosecutable norm. It introduces an inflexible definitional standard by which an illegal monopoly position would be determined. Over the years, the judicial determination of illegal market dominance has varied; from the rule of reason doctrine, to a 33 percent market share in the Philadelphia Girard case, and the more recent 7.5 percent share in the Von Grocery case.

More recently, the Small and Independent Business Protection Act was introduced for Congressional review in 1979. The proposal would establish an upper absolute bound on the size of firms engaged in merger activity and specifically prohibits a consolidation in which:

(1) The sales or assets of either firm exceeds 2 billion, or

(2) both companies possess assets or sales in excess of 350 million, or

(3) the sales or assets of one of the firms exceed 350 million, or other firm had a 20 percent or higher share of a 100 million sales market.

The proposal additionally specifies that firms would be exempt from prosecution if the merger substantially strengthens competition or contributes to measurable cost efficiencies.

While imperfect, the nation's regulatory policy has successfully established an enforcement standard which must be continually strengthened. It remains the least permissive and most restrictive of any policy directives pursued by any other country, and remains a meaningful expression of the nation's commitment to the competitive, free enterprise ideals.

INDEX

S

T

U

V

W

X

ABOUT THE AUTHOR

Kenneth Parzych is Professor of Economics at Eastern Connecticut State University. He is a graduate of American International College (B.A.), the University of New Hampshire (M.A.), and received the Ph.D degree from the University of Connecticut. Author of numerous journal articles dealing with antitrust laws, he has served as a consultant to numerous businesses and organizations, and has additionally served as a member of the Council of Economic Advisors to several Governors of the State of Connecticut.